"This new Sheinwold book has every attribute that appeals to me and should, I think, appeal to everyone interested in bridge.

It is authoritative.
It is comprehensive, including a full review of the requirements for bids in all situations.
It presents the fine points of bridge in the most palatable way, with bridge hands that teach lessons that can be applied to innumerable other hands arising in normal play."

from the Introduction by
Albert H. Morehead, Bridge Editor
THE NEW YORK TIMES

Alfred Sheinwold is a master player, author of six bestselling contract bridge books and co-author with Edgar Kaplan of the famous HOW TO PLAY WINNING BRIDGE. He is editor of *Bridge World* and his syndicated column appears in over 200 papers.

♠ ♠ ♠ ♠ ♠ ♠ ♠ ♠ ♠ ♠ ♠ ♠ ♠ ♠

A SHORT CUT TO WINNING BRIDGE

♡ ♡ ♡ ♡ ♡ ♡ ♡ ♡ ♡ ♡ ♡ ♡ ♡ ♡ ♡ ♡ ♡

MY 100 MOST INTERESTING BRIDGE HANDS

◇ ◇ ◇ ◇ ◇ ◇ ◇ ◇ ◇ ◇ ◇ ◇ ◇ ◇ ◇ ◇

BY ALFRED SHEINWOLD

♣ ♣ ♣ ♣ ♣ ♣ ♣ ♣ ♣ ♣ ♣ ♣ ♣ ♣ ♣

YOUR ASSURANCE OF QUALITY · BANTAM BOOKS · NEW YORK

A SHORT CUT TO WINNING BRIDGE

*A Bantam Book / published by arrangement with
Fleet Publishing Corporation*

PRINTING HISTORY
*Fleet edition published December 1961
Bantam edition published May 1963*

*Bantam Books are published by Bantam Books, Inc. Its trade-mark,
consisting of the words "Bantam Books" and the portrayal of a bantam, is registered in the United States Patent Office and in other
countries. Marca Registrada. Printed in the United States of America. Bantam Books, Inc., 271 Madison Ave., New York 16, N. Y.*

CONTENTS

INTRODUCTION

BY

ALBERT H. MOREHEAD

Bridge Editor of THE NEW YORK TIMES
Editor, Hoyle Up-to-Date—The Official Rules of Card Games

It is generally known among the bridge élite that of the "big" bridge columns, those syndicated nationally, the sprightliest and most readable is the one written by Alfred Sheinwold.

But this very knack of making difficult subjects both interesting to read about and easy to understand may obscure the fact that Mr. Sheinwold is one of the most profound of the bridge scholars, with a knowledge of bridge theory exceeded by no one.

This new Sheinwold book has every attribute that appeals to me and should, I think, appeal to everyone interested in bridge.

It is authoritative.

It is comprehensive, including a full review of the requirements for bids in all situations.

It presents the fine points of bridge in the most palatable way, with bridge hands that are intrinsically interesting and that also teach lessons that can be applied to innumerable other hands arising in normal play. Almost any time one plays bridge he is likely to encounter a situation in bidding or play that will be clear to him because of something he read in this book.

Not the least part of the book's charm for me is the group of essays on interesting aspects of bridge, some of them technical or instructive but others concerned simply with sidelights that would engross even a person who does not play bridge.

I am honored to have been giving this opportunity to congratulate Mr. Sheinwold on his new book and I am sure that all who read it will experience the same pleasure that I have felt, reading not only this book but the Sheinwold bridge articles over the course of the years.

ALBERT H. MOREHEAD

New York
1961

BIDDING SUMMARY

Most of the hands in this book are bid according to the principles of "Standard American"—the system used by more than fifty million bridge players throughout the Western world.

These basic principles are set forth in the pages that follow.

How to Value Your Hand

The easiest way to find the value of your hand is to count points:

each ace	4 points
each king	3 points
each queen	2 points
each jack	1 point

When bidding your own suit, add:

for a void suit	3 points
for a singleton	2 points
for a doubleton	1 point

When raising partner's suit, add:

for a void suit	5 points
for a singleton	3 points
for a doubleton	1 point

Reduce these short-suit values by one point if you raise your partner's suit with only three-card trump support.

Key Numbers

There are 40 points in the entire deck, 10 in each suit. You need approximately:

37 points for a grand slam
33 points for a small slam
30 points for game in a minor suit
26 points for game in a major suit or in notrump
18–25 points for a part score

Quick Tricks

Counting your points will help you bid accurately when you or your partner will be the declarer. But it is better to count your Quick Tricks when an opponent has opened the bidding, when you want to count the tricks you will win on defense, or when you are thinking of an opening bid of two in a suit.

A-K (of same suit)	2 Quick Tricks
A-Q (of same suit)	1½ Quick Tricks
Ace	1 Quick Trick
K-Q (of same suit)	1 Quick Trick
K-x	½ Quick Trick

(Other queens and jacks are useful, but are not counted as Quick Tricks.)

Opening Bid of 1 in a Suit

Points	What to Do
11 or less	Pass
12	Bid, with 3 Quick Tricks
13	Bid, with 2½ Q.T.
14 or more	Bid

Consider an opening bid in notrump when you have balanced distribution (no singleton or void suit, not more than one doubleton).

With more than 21 points, consider an opening bid of two —either in notrump or in a strong suit.

Exceptions

In third position, after two passes, open in a strong suit with 10 or 11 points. Shade bidding requirements by 1 point if you have length in spades or length in both major suits.

Which Suit to Bid

Any suit of 5 cards is biddable. A four-card suit headed by Q-J or better is biddable.

Any suit of 6 or more cards is *re*biddable. A five-card suit headed by Q-J or better is rebiddable.

If your hand calls for a bid, and you have only one suit of four or more cards, bid that suit.

If you have two suits of unequal length, bid the *longer* suit.

If you have two suits of equal length, bid the *higher* suit.

Exceptions

With equal length in spades and clubs, bid clubs first.

With three 4-card suits, make your first bid in a minor suit.

With a 4-card major and no other long suit, and with only 14 or 15 points, bid 1 ♣ or 1 ◊ (whichever is stronger) instead of your 4-card suit.

Responding to 1 of a Suit

Your Points	Your Response
0 to 5	Pass
6 to 10	Raise partner's suit with 4 or more trumps or with three trumps headed by queen or better.
	Bid a higher suit of your own.
	Bid 1 NT if you cannot raise or bid a higher suit.
10 or 11	Raise to 4 of partner's major suit—with 5 or more trumps and a side singleton or void suit.
11 or 12	Bid a suit of your own, whether higher or lower than partner's.
	At your next turn you will raise partner, bid a suit of your own, or bid notrump depending on how the bidding has gone and the nature of your hand.
13 to 15	Bid 2 NT (forcing to game) with balanced distribution and a stopper in each unbid suit.
13 to 16	Jump to 3 of partner's major suit (forcing to game)—with Q-x-x-x or better of his suit. If partner's suit is a minor, respond in a suit of your

own or make a jump response in no-trump.

16 or 17 Jump to 3 NT with 4-3-3-3 distribution and strength in all unbid suits. (Avoid this response with more than one ace. You may miss a slam.)

17 or 18 Bid two suits of your own before bidding game. (Mild slam invitation.)

19 or more Jump in suit of your own. (Forcing to game, and a mild slam invitation.)

Rebids by Opener

Count your points again and see what kind of opening bid you have:

12 to 16 points—*weak*
17 to 19 points—*middling*
20 points or more—*strong*

With a strong opening bid you will force to game even if your partner has made a weak response (6 to 10 points).

With a middling hand, you will invite a game but will not force to game.

With a weak hand, you will pass a weak response or will make a minimum rebid.

Add your own points to those shown by partner's response. If the total is surely below 26, look for a chance to pass below game.

If the total is in the area of 26 points, look for a fit in a major suit. If there is no such fit, bid toward game in notrump. Consider game in a minor suit only if at least one of the partnership hands is very unbalanced.

If the partnership total is well above 30 points, consider a slam. You will usually have a reasonable play for slam with 33 points and a fit in at least one suit.

When you have a choice of rebids, bid notrump to show balanced distribution; bid a suit to hint at unbalanced distribution. First choice is a raise in partner's major suit if you have four trumps, or three headed by queen or better. Next choice is a rebid of your own major, if your suit is rebiddable.

Rebids by Responder

Your Points	Your Second Response
6 to 10	Pass if opener shows a weak hand. Accept an invitation with 9 or 10 points; reject it with 6 or 7 points. Bid on toward game if partner shows 20 points or more.
11 to 12	Make a second response (trying for game) if opener shows a weak hand. Bid on to game if opener shows a middling hand. Suggest a slam if opener shows a strong hand.
13 or more	Make sure of game opposite a weak

hand. Suggest a slam opposite a middling hand. Make sure of slam opposite a strong hand.

Opening Notrump Bids

Notrump Distribution: 4-3-3-3, 4-4-3-2, or 5-3-3-2.

Stoppers: An opening bid of 1 NT promises strength in at least 3 suits. A bid of 2 NT or higher promises strength in all 4 suits.

Points	Notrump Bid
13 to 15	Bid suit; 1 NT later
16 to 18	Bid 1 NT
19 to 21	Bid suit; jump in NT later
22 to 24	Bid 2 NT (highly invitational, but not forcing to game)
25 to 27	Bid 3 NT
28 or more	Bid 2 of a suit; too strong for any opening bid in notrump.

Responding to 1 NT

Points	Your Response
0 to 7	Pass with balanced hand. Bid any 6-card or longer suit; bid a 5-card suit with unbalanced distribution.
8 or 9	Raise to 2 NT if balanced. Jump to 3 of a strong rebiddable major suit. Bid 2 ♣ (Stayman Convention) with a biddable major suit.
10 to 14	Jump to 3 NT with balanced distribution. Jump to 3 of a rebiddable major suit. Bid 2 ♣ with a biddable major suit.
15 or 16	Invite a small slam: Jump to 4 NT with balanced distribution; but jump to 3 of a suit first with unbalanced hand.
17 or 18	Make sure of reaching a small slam.
19 or more	Suggest a grand slam, and make sure of reaching a small slam.

Stayman Convention

In response to 1 NT, bid 2 ♣ when you have 8 or more points in high cards, with 4 cards in one or both majors. This bid does not promise a biddable club holding; it asks the opener to show a 4-card or longer major suit if he can.

The idea is to find out whether or not the partnership has a fit in a major suit. If not, they will be safe at either 2 NT or 3 NT.

After a response of 2 ♣, the opener looks for a major suit of 4 or more cards. If he has such a suit, he bids it; if he has both majors, he bids spades first and waits for a chance to show hearts later.

If the opener has no major suit, he makes a rebid of 2 ◇.

Responding to 2 NT

After an opening bid of 2 NT any response is forcing to game.

0 to 3	—Pass.
4 to 8	—Raise to 3 NT or bid a suit.
9 or 10	—Suggest a slam.
11 or more	—Make sure of a slam.

Responding to 3 NT

Any response is a slam try.

The Forcing 2-Bid

An opening bid of 2 in any suit is forcing to game.

This means that both partners agree to keep bidding until game is reached or until an opponent is doubled. (A player who passes before game is reached may forfeit his partner's confidence, but he is not compelled by law to keep bidding.)

Requirements for a 2-bid are:

- At least 4 Quick Tricks.
- At least 9 playing tricks.

In general, a 2-bid is based on at least one very powerful suit. If you have trouble counting your sure playing tricks, the hand is not worth an opening bid of 2. (Weaker hands should be opened with just one.)

Responding to a 2-Bid

Do not pass. Make the "negative" response of 2 NT with 0 to 6 points.

With 7 to 10 points, make a *positive* response—anything except 2 NT. Raise partner's suit

with trump support, bid a suit of your own, or jump to 3 NT.

With 11 points or more, make a positive response first and then keep bidding until slam is reached.

Rebids by Opener

Keep the bidding open until game is reached. No further jump bids are needed.

If partner has made a positive response, consider a slam.

Show a new suit if you have a two-suited hand.

Rebid your suit if you have a one-suited hand.

Raise partner if he shows a suit for which you have strong support.

Rebid in notrump if your hand is more or less balanced.

Slam Bidding

The Blackwood Convention is used to find out how many aces partner holds. After a bid of 4 NT:

Response	Number of Aces
5 ♣	0 or all 4
5 ◇	1
5 ♡	2
5 ♠	3

If this conventional response is followed by a bid of 5 NT, the partnership has all of the aces and the responder shows kings in the same way.

Response	Number of Kings
6 ♣	0
6 ◇	1
6 ♡	2
6 ♠	3
6 NT	4

Many experts prefer the Gerber Convention for the purpose of showing aces and kings. This is particularly useful after an opening bid of 1 NT or 2 NT.

A jump to 4 ♣ asks partner how many aces he holds:

Response	Number of Aces
4 ♦	0 or all 4
4 ♥	1
4 ♠	2
4 NT	3

If this is followed by a bid of 5 ♣, the partnership has all of the aces, and the response shows kings:

Response	Number of Kings
5 ♦	0
5 ♥	1
5 ♠	2
5 NT	3
6 ♣	4

The Blackwood or Gerber Convention is used when one member of the partnership can decide for or against a slam if he knows how many aces his partner holds.

Use the Blackwood Convention when you have powerful suits and unbalanced distribution. Avoid using it when you have two or more small cards in an unbid suit.

Experts use cue bids to get to slams far more frequently than they use Blackwood or Gerber. A cue bid suggests a slam and asks partner if he has extra strength.

The most common situation for a cue bid is after the open-er's major suit has been raised to three. This double raise shows strong trump support and 13 to 16 points. Opener may then suggest a slam by bidding a new suit.

This bid in a new suit, called a cue bid, promises the ace but does not promise length. The bidder is interested in a slam and wants to know whether or not his partner is interested.

The responder signs off by bidding the agreed suit if he has no aces or if he has already bid the full value of his hand. With extra strength, responder may bid a suit in which he has the ace.

Defensive Overcalls

When an opponent has opened the bidding you may want to bid a suit of your own to indicate a favorable opening lead to your partner or even to outbid the opponents. You need a strong suit for either purpose.

Overcall at the level of *one* with a strong suit of 5 or more cards worth at least 3 sure playing tricks.

Overcall at the level of *two* with a strong suit of 5 or more cards worth at least 4 sure playing tricks.

For a non-jump overcall you also need some reasonable amount of high-card strength; at least 1½ Quick Tricks for a bid of one, and at least 2 Quick Tricks for a bid of two. Don't overcall with a useless hand.

Jump Overcalls

Most experts use the jump overcall to show a strong suit but a poor hand. A typical holding would be six cards headed by K-Q-J or seven cards headed Q-J-10, with no side strength in either case.

The jump overcall may lead to a good sacrifice bid or may interfere with the other side's bidding. It also warns partner not to take your hand seriously for defensive help or for normal bidding purposes.

Some experts use the jump overcall to show a strong hand, needing only a little help to make a game. When playing with a new partner avoid using *any* kind of jump overcall unless you have agreed on what the meaning of such a bid is to be in your partnership.

Takeout Doubles

Normally, you double when you expect to defeat the opponent's contract. The double is sometimes used, however, to ask your partner to bid his longest suit. A double used for this purpose is called a takeout double.

A double is for takeout if the opponent's bid is 1, 2, or 3 of a suit (a double of a no-trump bid is meant mostly for penalties); and if the doubler's partner has not previously bid or doubled.

The most typical situation occurs when the opening bid is at your right. You have only one or two cards of the opponent's suit, with good help for each of the other suits. You want your partner to choose a suit.

The takeout double promises about the same strength as an opening bid, together with strength in all unbid suits. Sometimes the doubler lacks support for one of the unbid suits but has a strong suit of his own to bid after he has first doubled to show his strength.

Responding to a Double

In general, bid your best suit. If you have a choice, prefer to respond in a major suit rather than in a minor suit.

The weaker your hand, the more important it is to respond to your partner's takeout double. Pass the double only if your holding in the opponent's suit is so strong that you can expect to draw trumps and win more tricks than the opponents.

Show your strength in responding, as follows:

Points

0 to 8	Respond without a jump.
9 to 11	Jump in your best suit (invitational).
12 or 13	Bid the opponent's suit (forcing for one round, almost always reaches game).
14 or more	Bid the opponent's suit and jump at your next turn (forcing to game).

Avoid responding in notrump; your partner is going to some pains to find out your best suit. Bid notrump only with real strength in the opponent's suit and a total value of about 10 points. A jump to 2 NT should promise about 13 points.

Penalty Doubles

The most profitable doubles are of low contracts. By the time the opponents get up to a high contract they usually know what they are doing, but they sometimes take risks at low levels.

The most typical situation occurs when your partner opens the bidding with one of a suit and the next player overcalls at the level of one or two.

Double an overcall of 2 ◇ or lower with:

At least one trump trick.

At least 10 points in good defensive values.

Shortness in partner's bid suit.

At least 1½ Quick Tricks in the unbid suits.

A bid of 2 ♡ or higher becomes a game-going contract when doubled. Because of the risk of doubling an opponent into game, add 2 points or ½ Quick Trick to the requirements just listed before doubling a game-going contract.

When a contract is already game, your double will not turn a part score into a game contract. This does not, however, make your double free. Double a game contract only when you expect to defeat it by at least 2 tricks, including one trick or more in the trump suit itself.

Count your trump tricks at their full playing value. For example, count 3 tricks for K-J-10-x of trumps if you are behind the bidder.

Count your Quick Tricks in the side suits, but count only the ace in a suit of 6 or more cards.

When your partner has bid, count on him for:

2 or 3 tricks for an opening bid of 1 in a suit.

4 tricks for an opening bid of 1 NT.

1 to 2 tricks for a defensive overcall.

1 trick for a raise of your bid.

No trick at all for a shutout bid.

A double 1 NT asks partner to pass, not to take out the double.

If you expect to be on lead you need a long, strong suit to lead and establish, with enough Quick Tricks on the outside to bring in your suit.

If your partner will be on lead, you need 16 to 18 points, with strength in all four suits.

Lead-Directing Doubles

A double of 3 NT by the non-leader asks partner to lead:

The suit bid by the defenders (if only one suit was bid).

The suit bid by the doubler (if each defender has bid).

The first suit bid by dummy (if no defender has bid).

A double of a *slam* contract that the opponents have bid voluntarily calls for an *unusual* lead:

Not a suit bid by the doubler, not the trump suit, and not the only unbid suit (if any).

The suit requested is usually the first suit bid by dummy, but may occasionally be some other suit that the non-leader is able to ruff immediately.

Shutout Bids

An opening bid of 3 or more in a suit is a shutout bid, meant to shut the opponents out or, at any rate, to rob the opponents of bidding room.

A shutout bid should be based on a long and strong suit, preferably topless—without any side strength.

The typical opening bid of three in a suit is made with a 7-card suit headed by Q-J-10 if not vulnerable or K-Q-J if vulnerable.

The typical opening bid of four in a suit is based on an 8-card suit or a freakish hand with 7-4 or 6-5 distribution in two suits.

Partner should avoid raising a shutout bid unless he can visualize a game opposite the typical weak hand shown by the bid.

Sacrifice Bids

The value of a game, including the trick score, is roughly 500 points. The value of a slam is about 1000 or 1500 points, depending on vulnerability.

If your opponents can bid and make a game, you lose nothing by overbidding and allowing them to collect a penalty of 500 points. A sacrifice bid that costs only 200 points or 300 points is a paying bid if the opponents have an easily biddable and makable game.

Beware of sacrificing against a game that is unbiddable or that the opponent is not skillful enough to make. Don't make sacrifice bids when you have a weak partner.

Modern Bidding Conventions

Blackwood Convention: See page 7.

Gerber Convention: See page 8.

Stayman Convention: See page 6.

Fishbein Convention: When your right-hand opponent bids 3 of a suit (shutout bid), you bid the next-higher suit for takeout. Partner may pass with a very weak hand and considerable length in the suit you have bid.

The advantage of the Fishbein Convention is that the double is used for penalties rather than for takeout. This may be useful when your opponents frequently make 3-bids on very ragged suits.

Some experts use the cheaper minor suit for takeout rather than the next higher suit. Over an opening bid of 3 ♣ they bid 3 ◇ for takeout; over any other 3-bid, they bid 4 ♣ for takeout.

Weak 2-bids: The opening bid of 2 ♠, 2 ♡, or 2 ◇ shows a strong suit of 6 cards, with slightly less than the strength of a normal opening bid.

Partner needs somewhat more than the strength of an opening bid to visualize a game.

The opening bid of 2 ♣ is reserved for all forcing 2-bids. The negative response is 2 ◇, after which the opener shows his true suit.

Texas Convention: After an opening bid of 1 NT, responder jumps to 4 ◇ to show length in hearts; to 4 ♡ to show length in spades. Opener is supposed to bid the next higher suit to play the hand in the right contract.

The advantage is that the strong hand is concealed and gets the benefit of the opening lead. The disadvantage is that even experts tend to forget the convention and wind up playing the hand in a ridiculous contract.

Drury Convention: If partner opens 1 ♠ or 1 ♡ in third or fourth position, you bid 2 ♣ to show a good hand and to ask partner to state whether or not

he has a sound opening bid.

The opener makes a rebid of 2 ◇ to show a sub-normal hand; and makes any other descriptive bid to show a sound opening bid.

Weak Notrumps: The opening bid of 1 NT shows about 11 to 14 points and balanced distribution (instead of the standard value of 16 to 18 points). Responder needs at least 12 points to try for game. (The weak notrump is the corner-stone of the Kaplan-Sheinwold System, fully explained in *How to Play Winning Bridge,* by Edgar Kaplan and Alfred Sheinwold.)

Landy Convention: Bid 2 ♣ over an opponent's opening bid of 1 NT to request takeout in a major suit. The bid is most effective against the weak notrump, but may be used instead against the standard notrump.

When 2 ♣ is bid for takeout, the double may be used to show a stronger hand—preferably for penalties.

Five-Card Majors: Some experts promise a suit of five or more cards with any opening bid of 1 ♠ or 1 ♡. The opening bid of 1 ♣ or 1 ◇ is frequently based on a 3-card suit when this method is followed.

When you begin to play a notrump hand, count the tricks that you can win without giving up the lead.

If you can run your tricks without fuss or effort, you do so first and think about it later.

If you must give up the lead to develop the tricks needed for your contract, think ahead to see what damage the opponents may do to you when they gain the lead.

The Hold-Up

The hold-up play is one of your basic tools to prevent an opponent from defeating you with his long suit.

The idea is to refuse to win the first trick in a suit. You hold up your winner for a trick or two. If your plan is successful, you take your trick just as one of the opponents plays his last card in the suit.

Later on, that opponent will be unable to lead his partner's long suit.

In the typical hold-up you have the ace of an opponent's long suit. You postpone winning your ace until the second or third round of the suit.

As we see, however, in the first few hands, you may have to hold up with a double stopper or at the cost of a possible second trick in the enemy's long suit.

The third hand shows that the hold-up play is sometimes wrong. You must occasionally win the first trick in the enemy's long suit.

The Dangerous Opponent

In many hands, whether played at a trump suit or at notrump, one opponent is dangerous and the other may safely be allowed to win a trick.

Your first step in playing such hands correctly is to note the difference between the two opponents. The next step is to manage your affairs so as to keep the dangerous opponent out of the lead.

The simplest device is to take your finesses through the dangerous opponent, as in Hand No. 8. If the finesse wins, well and good; if it loses, the trick goes to the safe opponent.

Which Suit?

In some notrump hands your problem is to develop the correct suit first. This is not always the longest suit in the partnership hands.

Sometimes you must begin with the suit that forces a dangerous opponent to win a trick before he has established his long suit. If you must face an enemy, do so before he is fully armed.

Sometimes you must count your tricks and must begin with the suit that will produce the number of tricks required for your contract. These may be sure tricks, as in Hand No. 5, or possible tricks, as in No. 6.

In Hand No. 7 we see a combination of ideas. The problem is to begin on the right suit, but this is combined with the principle of shutting out the dangerous opponent.

When to Finesse

Most bridge players will automatically take any finesse that presents itself. Sooner or later they discover that there is no Santa Claus.

Some finesses must be refused because you can't afford to lose to the dangerous opponent. As we see in Hand No. 10, the missing honor may drop if you decide not to finesse.

This idea is developed a little further in No. 11. When you can take only one of two finesses, you can improve your chances by trying for the drop in one suit before trying the finesse in the other.

In some cases you refuse a finesse because you don't need it. If the finesse wins, it gives you only an unimportant extra trick; if it loses, it costs you the contract. The principle is shown in Hand No. 13.

Entries

The right to lead may be very important, and much of the skill in bridge consists in winning your tricks in the right hand at the right time. A card that wins a trick is called an *entry,* and experts pay much attention to *entry management.*

In Hand No. 15 declarer must create an extra entry to dummy by getting rid of a high card from his hand. This does not give him an additional trick in the suit itself; but it allows him to reach dummy and thus develop an additional trick in a different suit.

A similar principle is shown in No. 16. Here, declarer must resist the temptation of a free finesse. If you begin your meal with the ice cream, somebody may walk off with the steak.

Advanced Plays

The last four notrump hands present advanced plays for our study.

No. 17 is a safety play. There are certain ways of playing a suit to avoid excessive loss, as we see in the handling of the diamonds.

In No. 18 and No. 19 we see a play that goes under various names—the end-play, the throw-in, elimination, strip play, etc. What's in a name? It smells sweet, whatever you call it.

The idea is to remove safe "out" cards from an opponent's hand and then throw him into the lead. If you have done your preliminary work thoroughly, the opponent must now make you a present of a trick no matter what card he leads back.

No. 20 shows a simple squeeze. It isn't necessary to know how to squeeze an opponent, but it's very impressive. Your opponent suddenly discovers that he must lose a trick no matter what he discards; and he looks at you with a new respect.

1. A SIMPLE HOLD-UP

A hold-up play is meant to cut the communications between your two opponents. Sometimes you must give up a possible trick in the process of holding up.

North dealer
Both sides vulnerable

NORTH
♠ 7 4 3
♡ K 9
♢ A K 9 8 4
♣ A 8 2

WEST
♠ A 10 8 6 2
♡ 10 4 3
♢ 6 2
♣ Q J 7

EAST
♠ J 9
♡ Q J 6 5 2
♢ Q 7 3
♣ 10 6 5

SOUTH
♠ K Q 5
♡ A 8 7
♢ J 10 5
♣ K 9 4 3

North	East	South	West
1 ◇	Pass	2 NT	Pass
3 NT	Pass	Pass	Pass

Opening lead — ♠ 6

West opens the six of spades, and East plays the jack.

Perhaps your first instinct is to take the king or queen of spades and think about the matter later. If so, you had better do something about your instincts.

If you win the first trick, you must go after diamonds and allow East to win a trick with the queen. East then returns his other spade, and West can take four spade tricks, defeating the contract.

Refuse First Trick

The correct play is to refuse the first trick. East leads his other spade, and you play the queen. West takes the ace of spades and gives you a spade trick.

Now you go after the diamonds. You lead the jack of diamonds for a finesse, not caring too much whether the finesse wins or loses. The important thing is that West cannot win the trick, and only West is dangerous.

As it happens, East wins the trick with the queen of diamonds. What can he do? His spades are gone, thanks to your hold-up play, and East's other suits are harmless. No matter what East does, you can take nine tricks with the long diamonds and top cards.

What would happen if East had three spades, instead of only two? In that case, East would win the first trick with the jack of spades, and you would be allowed to win the second trick with the queen of spades. Later on, East would get in with the queen of diamonds to lead his last spade. Nevertheless, the opponents would take only *three* spade tricks and one diamond, and you would still make your contract.

2. THE HOLD-UP WITH TWO STOPPERS

When you hold two sure tricks in the suit that has been opened, should you take one of your tricks at once, or should you hold up?

North dealer
North-South vulnerable

NORTH
♠ 10 6
♡ A Q J
◇ Q J 10 9 7
♣ A J 10

WEST	EAST
♠ J 9 7 5 3 2	♠ K 8
♡ 7 3	♡ 9 8 5 4 2
◇ K 8 5	◇ A
♣ 5 2	♣ 9 7 6 4 3

SOUTH
♠ A Q 4
♡ K 10 6
◇ 6 4 3 2
♣ K Q 8

North	East	South	West
1 ◇	Pass	2 NT	Pass
3 NT	All Pass		

Opening lead — ♠ 5

West leads the five of spades, and East plays the king. What should you do?

The correct play is to refuse the first trick. Your intention is to exhaust one opponent's cards in the dangerous suit.

East leads his other spade at the second trick, and you win. Now East is out of spades, so your hold-up play has done its job.

You need one diamond trick for your contract. Whenever you lead diamonds, East cannot lead a spade. You can win any return very comfortably, and then you can knock out the king of diamonds. You win ten tricks.

What would happen if West had both the ace and king of diamonds? You would be defeated. When a hand is really unlucky, all you can do is reach for the crying towel.

You would lose your game contract if you won the first trick with the ace of spades. You would have to lead a diamond pretty soon, and East would take the ace of diamonds and would return his other spade.

At this stage it would be too late for you to think of a hold-up play. If you refused the second spade trick, West would win with the jack of spades and lead a third spade. This would establish the rest of West's suit, and he would get in with the king of diamonds in time to defeat the contract.

A Word of Warning

Before you start to hold up your tricks left and right, consider a word of warning. If the opponents open one of your strong suits, you may have to win immediately for fear that they will be bright enough to switch to your weakest suit.

The time to hold up is when the opponents open a suit that represents a real threat.

3. BLOCK THEIR SUIT

Avoid a hold-up play when you know that the opponent's suit is going to block.

South dealer
Both sides vulnerable

NORTH
♠ A 4
♡ J 8 6
◇ Q 3 2
♣ K Q J 8 5

WEST
♠ Q J 8 6 3
♡ 7 5 4 2
◇ 5 4
♣ A 6

EAST
♠ K 10
♡ Q 10 9 3
◇ 10 8 7 6
♣ 7 3 2

SOUTH
♠ 9 7 5 2
♡ A K
◇ A K J 9
♣ 10 9 4

South	West	North	East
1 ◇	Pass	2 ♣	Pass
2 NT	Pass	3 NT	All Pass

Opening lead — ♠ 6

West leads the six of spades. Should you take the ace or should you hold up?

You have nothing to worry about if the spades are divided 4–3. Somebody may take three spade tricks and the ace of clubs, but you will then take the rest of the tricks. You do have something to worry about if the spades break 5–2, for then somebody may take *four* spade tricks and the ace of clubs.

Assume the worst—that East has only two spades. They must both be honor cards (10 or higher). Otherwise, West's long suit would be headed by three honors, in which case his opening lead would be an honor rather than a low card.

This steers you to the right play. You put up dummy's ace of spades immediately. East's best play is to drop the king of spades, but it won't help him.

You lead clubs, forcing out the ace. West can take the queen and jack of spades, but then your nine of spades will stop the suit. If East hadn't dropped his king, he would have to win the second spade trick, and then the defenders would get one trick less.

Hold-Up Loses

In this situation, a hold-up play loses. For example, suppose you refuse the first trick. East wins with the king of spades and returns his other spade to dummy's ace. Now the suit is unblocked. When West takes the ace of clubs he is ready to cash the rest of the spades.

Look for this sort of blocking play whenever you have A-x in one hand and any four low cards in the other hand. You are safest when your four cards are headed by the 10 or the 9-8, but in a pinch *any* four cards may do the trick.

4. FORCE OUT THE ENTRY

When you must tackle two suits, which should you begin with? As a rule, start with the suit in which the dangerous opponent may have a card of entry.

North dealer
North-South vulnerable

```
                NORTH
              ♠ 9 3
              ♡ Q 9 6
              ◇ A K 7 5
              ♣ A Q J 4
WEST                      EAST
♠ Q 10 8 4 2              ♠ J 7 5
♡ A 5                     ♡ 8 7 3 2
◇ 9 4 3                   ◇ Q 10 8 2
♣ 8 7 2                   ♣ K 5
                SOUTH
              ♠ A K 6
              ♡ K J 10 4
              ◇ J 6
              ♣ 10 9 6 3
```

North	East	South	West
1 ◇	Pass	1 ♡	Pass
2 ♣	Pass	2 NT	Pass
3 NT	Pass	Pass	Pass

Opening lead — ♠ 4

West opened the four of spades, and South won with the king. South needed tricks in both hearts and clubs, and he had to decide which suit to tackle first.

South went after hearts first because West, the opponent with the long spades, might have the ace of hearts. If West held the king of clubs, that card would not win a trick for him.

West Entryless

West refused the first heart, hoping that his partner could win. West had to take the second heart, however, and now his hand was entryless. He led another spade, and South refused the trick. South took the next spade, thus running East out of spades.

Declarer could now safely afford to try the club finesse. East won with the king of clubs but couldn't lead a spade and couldn't find any other way to get to the West hand. South easily won the rest of the tricks, making his contract and an overtrick.

Now see what happens if South tackles the *clubs* first instead of the hearts. East wins with the king of clubs and can return a spade. This allows West to establish the rest of his suit, regardless of whether or not South holds up. South must eventually tackle the hearts, and West takes the ace of hearts and defeats the contract with the rest of the spades.

5. COUNT YOUR TRICKS

Are you a speculative bridge player, or do you keep an eye out for sure things? There's more excitement in speculation, more security in the sure thing. You pays your money and you takes your choice.

North dealer
North-South vulnerable

NORTH
♠ K 9 2
♡ 8 6 3
◇ A K J 8 4
♣ Q 10

WEST	EAST
♠ 6 4 3	♠ Q J 10 8
♡ J 10 9 4 2	♡ 7 5
◇ 7 2	◇ Q 10 9 5
♣ 5 4 2	♣ A K 7

SOUTH
♠ A 7 5
♡ A K Q
◇ 6 3
♣ J 9 8 6 3

North	East	South	West
1 ◇	Pass	2 NT	Pass
3 NT	All Pass		

Opening lead — ♡ J

South was a born speculator so he won the first heart trick and tried the diamond finesse. Diamonds may be a girl's best friend, but South was no girl. The finesse lost, and things went from bad to worse.

East returned the queen of spades, and South was in trou-ble. It was too late to switch to clubs, for East would get two clubs, two spades, and one diamond. Instead, South continued with the diamonds, but he could get only eight tricks.

East took his second diamond trick and led the jack of spades to knock out declarer's last stopper in that suit. Now South could cash his eight tricks, but East took the rest.

Clubs Are Safe

South should win the first heart and lead *clubs* instead of diamonds. East can take the king of clubs and force out the king of spades. Declarer now knocks out the ace of clubs while still controlling each suit. He can surely win two spades, three hearts, two diamonds, and three clubs.

If you like sure things, your best course is to count tricks at the beginning of the play and tackle the suit that guarantees the contract. Be sure to estimate the damage the opponents can do each time you give them the lead.

If you prefer excitement, don't bother to count your tricks or make a plan for the play of the hand. You'll have the excitement, and your opponents will have the tricks!

In many notrump contracts each side races to set up and cash its long suit. If you see the opponents are going to win the race you must look for a short cut.

South dealer
Both sides vulnerable

NORTH
♠ 6 2
♡ K 4
♢ Q 10 6 5 2
♣ J 10 8 4

WEST
♠ J 8 7 4
♡ J 9 2
♢ J 9 7 4
♣ K 3

EAST
♠ K 10 9 5 3
♡ Q 10 8 6 3
♢ A
♣ 7 5

SOUTH
♠ A Q
♡ A 7 5
♢ K 8 3
♣ A Q 9 6 2

South	West	North	East
1 ♣	Pass	1 ♢	Pass
2 NT	Pass	3 NT	All Pass

Opening lead — ♠ 4

West leads the four of spades, East puts up the king, and you win with the ace. Your normal plan is to lead a heart to the king and return the jack of clubs for a finesse. If the finesse succeeds, you have five clubs, two hearts and two spades—nine fast tricks.

What if the club finesse loses? Back comes another spade, and you have only eight tricks. Then the opponents win the race,

since they will be in position to take three spades, one club and one diamond.

Try Diamonds

The only possible short cut is in diamonds. If you lead a small diamond from one hand or the other, and the next player has the ace of diamonds you may be able to win the race.

If the opponent plays low, you can steal the diamond trick and then switch back to clubs. You will then make four sure clubs, one diamond, two hearts and two spades.

If the opponent steps up with the ace of diamonds, you can try for four diamond tricks. And if the jack of diamonds fails to drop, you can try the club finesse. You cannot be worse off than if you had tried the clubs from the start, and if the diamonds work you will be better off.

The best plan is to reach dummy with a heart and lead a low diamond from dummy. You cannot tell which opponent has the ace of diamonds or which opponent is short in diamonds, but you can cope with the singleton ace of diamonds only if East has it.

East must take the ace of diamonds and return a spade. You take the queen of spades, cash the king of diamonds, discovering that East has no more, and then finesse through West's diamonds to run the rest of the suit.

7. DEVELOP THE RIGHT SUIT

How do you choose the right suit to develop? Do you set to work on your longest suit, or is there some other basis for your choice?

South dealer
North-South vulnerable

NORTH
♠ J 6
♡ A 3 2
♢ 10 8 5 3
♣ K J 4 3

WEST
♠ K 10 7 5 2
♡ Q 9 5 4
♢ Q 4
♣ 8 7

EAST
♠ 9 4 3
♡ 10 8 7
♢ K 7 6 2
♣ Q 10 9

SOUTH
♠ A Q 8
♡ K J 6
♢ A J 9
♣ A 6 5 2

South	West	North	East
1 ♣	Pass	2 ♣	Pass
3 NT	All Pass		

Opening lead — ♠ 5

West opened the five of spades, and South very properly put up dummy's jack. East played low, and dummy's jack of spades held the trick.

Now what?

South was tempted to go after the clubs, the longest and strongest suit in the combined hands. After some thought, however, declarer led a low diamond from the dummy and finessed the jack from his own hand.

The finesse lost to West's queen, but West was not overjoyed. West didn't want to lead a spade to declarer's ace-queen. If he returned a heart or a diamond, South would get a free finesse.

West finally decided to lead a club. This was lucky for him, since any other lead would cost West a trick immediately.

Continues Plan

South continued his plan of developing the diamonds. He put up dummy's king of clubs and led another diamond, finessing the nine from his hand. South was willing to lose the finesse, for then dummy's ten of diamonds would become established. Moreover, West would be unable to do any harm.

As it happened, the second finesse in diamonds worked. Now South could afford to take the ace of clubs and give up a trick to the queen of clubs.

Back came a spade, and South could easily take his tricks. He was sure to win two spades, two hearts, two diamonds and three clubs. If he play the hand very shrewdly he might even make an extra trick, but the contract at any rate was on ice.

Now we can see why South decided to work on the *diamonds* first. He could steer the lead to *West*, who could do no damage. If South went after the *clubs* first, *East* would gain the lead and would return a spade. This would give South serious trouble and might even lead to the defeat of the contract.

When only one of the opponents is dangerous, you must try to keep him out of the lead.

South dealer
Neither side vulnerable

NORTH
♠ Q 6
♡ A 10 6 5
◇ K 9 8
♣ K 8 7 3

WEST
♠ J 9 7 3 2
♡ 7 4
◇ Q 7 6 2
♣ Q 4

EAST
♠ A 10 4
♡ Q J 9 8 2
◇ 4
♣ J 10 9 5

SOUTH
♠ K 8 5
♡ K 3
◇ A J 10 5 3
♣ A 6 2

South	West	North	East
1 ◇	Pass	1 ♡	Pass
1 NT	Pass	3 NT	All Pass

Opening lead — ♠ 3

West opens the three of spades, and you hopefully play the queen from dummy. To your disappointment, East produces the ace of spades, winning the trick.

East continues with the ten of spades, and you refuse the trick. You take the third spade trick with the king.

By this time you know that West has led from a long suit. He is the dangerous opponent, since he will take the rest of his spades if he gains the lead.

East is not dangerous, because he has no spades to lead.

Two-Way Finesse

Now that you know which opponent is dangerous you can shut the door in his face. The two-way finesse in diamonds gives you your chance.

After taking the king of spades you lead the jack of diamonds from your hand. West plays low, and you allow the jack to ride for a finesse. If East had the queen, he would win a trick, but you wouldn't mind giving this trick to the safe opponent.

As it happens, your finesse works. You lead another diamond to finesse dummy's nine. Then you take the king of diamonds and return to your hand to lead out the ace of diamonds. Your contract is then safe.

You would finesse in the opposite direction if dummy's queen of spades won the first trick. Then *East* would be the dangerous opponent, and West would be safe.

If that were the case you would cash the king of diamonds at once and then lead the nine of diamonds for a finesse through East. That would keep East out of the lead.

When you can finesse in either direction, choose the direction that keeps the dangerous opponent out. You may not win the finesse, but at least you'll be safe.

9. GIVE TRICK TO SAFE OPPONENT

Variety is the spice of bridge. Unusual circumstances may compel you to handle a familiar combination of cards in an unfamiliar way. Problems of this kind give the game much of its appeal.

South dealer
Both sides vulnerable

NORTH
♠ 7 3 2
♡ Q 9 5
♢ K Q 8 3
♣ Q 9 4

WEST
♠ Q J 10 9 6
♡ K J 3
♢ 5 4
♣ A J 8

EAST
♠ 8 4
♡ 8 7 6 2
♢ J 10 9 6 2
♣ 10 7

SOUTH
♠ A K 5
♡ A 10 4
♢ A 7
♣ K 6 5 3 2

South	West	North	East
1♣	1♠	Pass	Pass
1 NT	Pass	2 NT	Pass
3 NT	All Pass		

Opening lead — ♠ Q

West opened the queen of spades, and South refused the first trick. West continued with the jack of spades, and South won.

Declarer counted his tricks and saw that he needed three clubs. The question was how to develop the suit properly.

It was clear from the bidding that West held the ace of clubs. The "normal" way to play the clubs, therefore, was to lead a low club to the queen and then return a club. South would play low, hoping that West's ace would fall on the trick willy-nilly.

Play Would Fail

This play would fail as the cards were distributed. West would win the second club with the jack and would establish his spades. He would gain the lead with the ace of clubs to run his good spades, taking three spades and two clubs.

South felt sure that West had started with a five-card spade suit for his overcall. This meant that East was out of spades. Therefore South led a low club from his hand and finessed dummy's nine.

East had to win the club trick and couldn't lead a spade. South still had to lose two clubs in all, but the opponents didn't have time to establish the spades.

East returned a heart, and South put up the ace. He led another low club, and West was helpless to defeat the contract. The defenders could get two clubs, one spade and one heart, but South had the rest.

10. MOTHER'S RULE FOR FINESSES

"When I was a little boy," said South, after he had played today's hand, "my mother taught me the first rule of bridge: Never take a finesse when the king is singleton!"

"Very funny," said East.

South dealer
North-South vulnerable

NORTH
♠ 7 4
♡ Q 10 4
♢ A Q J 8 5
♣ K 10 8

WEST
♠ A 10 8 5 2
♡ 6 5 3
♢ 7 6 3 2
♣ 4

EAST
♠ J 9 3
♡ K J 9 2
♢ K
♣ 7 6 5 3 2

SOUTH
♠ K Q 6
♡ A 8 7
♢ 10 9 4
♣ A Q J 9

South	West	North	East
1 NT	Pass	3 NT	All Pass

Opening lead — ♠ 5

West led the five of spades, East put up the jack, and South won with the queen. South saw that he needed the diamonds. His first impulse was to take a finesse, but then he thought of his mother. So he led a diamond to dummy's ace, capturing East's king.

The rest was, of course, very easy. South took the first eleven tricks. If he had taken the diamond finesse, he would have lost to the king; and then a spade return would have allowed West to take four spade tricks.

Simple Explanation

There is a simple explanation of South's unusual play in diamonds. His mother never actually played bridge. Nor did he peek into East's hand. He just made the correct play, and it happened to pay off.

South cannot afford to lose a diamond trick to *East*. He can afford to lose a trick to *West,* for West cannot safely lead a second spade.

How can you shut East out if he has the king of diamonds? You can't if the king is guarded. The only insurance you can take out is to play the ace first, just in case East's king is unguarded.

If the king drops, be sure to give your mother credit for the fine play.

When you take a finesse you have an even chance to gain a trick. You also have an even chance to lose the finesse. If you have a choice between two finesses, how do you know which to take? Isn't one even chance as good as another?

South dealer
North-South vulnerable

NORTH
♠ 10 5
♡ A J 8 6
♢ K 8 5
♣ K 7 3 2

WEST
♠ K Q J 9 7
♡ 5 4
♢ Q 2
♣ Q 9 8 6

EAST
♠ 8 6 4 3
♡ K 7 3 2
♢ 7 4 3
♣ J 10

SOUTH
♠ A 2
♡ Q 10 9
♢ A J 10 9 6
♣ A 5 4

South	West	North	East
1 ♢	1 ♠	2 ♢	Pass
2 NT	Pass	3 NT	All Pass

Opening lead — ♠ K

Put yourself in South's shoes. You win the first or second spade trick and wonder whether to finesse in hearts or in diamonds.

If the heart finesse wins, you have a spade, four hearts, two diamonds and two clubs—nine of the best. If you decide to try the diamonds instead, and happen to guess right, you have a spade, a heart, five diamonds, and two clubs.

Which suit should you try? If you decide to finesse in diamonds, which way do you finesse?

Combination Shot

Your best chance is to try a combination shot. First try to drop the missing honor in one of the red suits; and then, if it doesn't drop, try the finesse in the other suit. This gives you two chances instead of only one.

Which card is more likely to drop—the king of hearts or the queen of diamonds? The answer is very obvious.

Therefore you lay down the king and ace of diamonds as a starter. If the queen fails to drop, you will be in position to try the heart finesse.

As it happens, however, the queen of diamonds does drop. Thereupon you take your nine tricks and score the game and rubber. No finesse is necessary.

12. DUCK A TRICK TO SAFE OPPONENT

Ducking may keep the dangerous opponent out of the lead.

South dealer
Both sides vulnerable

NORTH
♠ 7 4
♡ A K 5 4
♢ 8 7 4 3
♣ A Q 6

WEST
♠ K J 9 6 3
♡ J 10 8
♢ J 10 6
♣ 7 3

EAST
♠ Q 8 5
♡ Q 9 3
♢ Q 5
♣ 9 8 5 4 2

SOUTH
♠ A 10 2
♡ 7 6 2
♢ A K 9 2
♣ K J 10

South	West	North	East
1 ♢	Pass	1 ♡	Pass
1 NT	Pass	3 NT	All Pass

Opening lead — ♠ 6

West opens the six of spades, and East plays the queen. You refuse the first and second spade tricks.

When you take the third trick with the ace of spades you know that West has led from a long suit. He is the dangerous opponent, since he will take the rest of his spades if he is permitted to win another trick. East is the safe opponent, since he is now out of spades.

You have eight tricks in top cards, and your problem is to develop an extra heart or an extra diamond without allowing West to gain the lead. You plan to duck a trick to East.

Must Reach Dummy

Diamonds are your main hope, but you must reach dummy to lead diamonds through East. If you lead a *low* diamond from your own hand, West will win the trick; and if you lead a *high* diamond from your hand, East will get rid of his queen of diamonds like a hot potato.

You lead a heart toward dummy, and West plays the eight. Too bad. If West had played the three of hearts you would have ducked then and there, allowing East to win the trick. You can't afford to play low from dummy on the *eight* of hearts, for West will win and take his spades.

Having arrived in dummy with the king of hearts, you return a low diamond. If East plays the queen, you are ready to duck—allowing East to win with his queen. Assume that East plays low; you win with the ace of diamonds.

Now you get back to dummy with a club and lead another diamond through East. This time East is obliged to play his queen. You play low from your hand, allowing East to win.

The idea is to give up one diamond trick, but to make sure to give it up to the *safe* opponent. This puts you in position to take the next diamond with the king, after which your last diamond will be good for your ninth trick.

When a bridge player goes to heaven, he can be sure that his finesses will all win. While he stays on earth, however, he must consider the possibility that a finesse may lose. This may have a bearing on his plan for the hand.

North dealer
North-South vulnerable

NORTH
♠ 5 2
♡ A J 4
♢ K Q J 9 3
♣ K J 5

WEST	EAST
♠ A K 8 7	♠ 9 4 3
♡ 9 5	♡ K 8 7 6 2
♢ 6 4 2	♢ A 8 7
♣ 8 6 3 2	♣ 9 7

SOUTH
♠ Q J 10 6
♡ Q 10 3
♢ 10 5
♣ A Q 10 4

North	East	South	West
1 ♢	Pass	1 ♠	Pass
2 ♢	Pass	2 NT	Pass
3 NT	Pass	Pass	Pass

Opening lead — ♡ 9

West opened the nine of hearts and South blithely finessed, perhaps thinking he had already arrived in heaven. If so, he soon found out that he was in quite a different place.

East won the first trick with the king of hearts and returned the four of spades. South had to put up the ten of spades, and West won with the king. West returned the seven of spades, East put up the nine, and South won with the jack.

Doomed by Diamonds

At this point South could expect to win a spade, two hearts, and four clubs. He needed the diamonds for his contract. When he led a diamond, however, East took the ace of diamonds and led his last spade. This gave West two spade tricks, defeating the game contract.

Now see what happens if South decides against the finesse at the first trick. He goes right up with the ace of hearts and leads diamonds to drive out the ace. This puts South in position to win four diamonds, four clubs, and the ace of hearts. The defenders can take the king of hearts, the ace of diamonds, and two top spades, but this is not enough to defeat the contract.

If you had X-ray eyes, you could win at bridge without being a good player. If your vision is only normal, however, it won't hurt you to play the cards skillfully.

North dealer
North-South vulnerable

NORTH
♠ K 10 4
♡ A K 7
◇ K Q 8 7 3
♣ 9 7

WEST
♠ 7 5
♡ 10 9 5 4 2
◇ A
♣ 8 6 5 4 3

EAST
♠ A J 9 8 3
♡ 8 3
◇ J 6
♣ Q J 10 2

SOUTH
♠ Q 6 2
♡ Q J 6
◇ 10 9 5 4 2
♣ A K

North	East	South	West
1 ◇	1 ♠	1 NT	Pass
2 NT	Pass	3 NT	Pass
Pass	Pass		

Opening lead — ♠ 7

West opens the seven of spades, and you must try to make sure of nine tricks without seeing the hands of the two opponents. How should you go about this?

Suppose you play a low spade from dummy. East finesses the eight, and you win with the queen. You hope that East has the ace of diamonds, and you lead a diamond to force out the ace.

This play doesn't work. West turns up with the ace of diamonds and leads another spade. East takes four more spade tricks, defeating the contract.

Let's try another way of playing the hand. You play low from the dummy at first trick, and East finesses the eight. You refuse the first trick. East continues with the ace and then a low spade.

Now, *as the cards lie,* you make your contract. West has the ace of diamonds but cannot lead another spade. Your hold-up play at the first trick has saved your contract.

Don't congraulate yourself. You would lose the hand if *East* had the ace of diamonds. You have just guessed right, or perhaps you have used X-ray eyes.

Correct Play

If you use the correct play, you don't need a crystall ball or an X-ray machine. Just put up the *king* of spades from dummy at the first trick, and you don't care which opponent has the ace of diamonds.

If East wins the first trick with the ace of spades, he cannot afford to lead another spade. (You would allow a small spade to ride to dummy's ten.) This gives you time to knock out the ace of diamonds, no matter where it may be. If East refuses the first trick, you still have the suit stopped. Either way, you are safe.

"These young players are all very careless," said the Old Kibitzer. "In my day, we played the right card instead of the card nearest the thumb."

South dealer
North-South vulnerable

NORTH
♠ 7 5 3 2
♡ A 8 4
◇ J 7 2
♣ 7 3 2

WEST
♠ Q 10 8 4
♡ 7 6
◇ Q 9 8 5 3
♣ 9 6

EAST
♠ J 9
♡ 10 9 5 3 2
◇ A 6
♣ K 10 8 4

SOUTH
♠ A K 6
♡ K Q J
◇ K 10 4
♣ A Q J 5

South	West	North	East
2 NT	Pass	3 NT	All Pass

Opening lead — ◇ 5

West opened the five of diamonds, and East played the ace. South "carelessly" dropped the king of diamonds, and the Old Kibitzer got up from his seat and walked across the club to kibitz at another table.

As you might imagine, the Old Kibitzer was wrong. South was correct in playing the king of diamonds.

South needed three club tricks to make his contract. For this purpose, he wanted to lead clubs twice from the dummy.

How could declarer get to dummy twice? The ace of hearts was one entry, but where was the other?

The jack of diamonds was the other entry—but only if South got rid of the king.

Let's see how it worked out. East returned his six of diamonds at the second trick, and West won with the queen. Now South could get to dummy with the jack of diamonds to lead a club.

South naturally finessed the queen of clubs, winning the trick. He got back to dummy with the ace of hearts to lead another club. This time he finessed the jack of clubs, winning the finesse once more.

Now South had nine easy tricks: two spades, three hearts, one diamond and three clubs.

Stinginess Doesn't Pay

South would lose his game contract if he made the stingy play at the first trick. Suppose South plays a low diamond instead of the king. East returns a diamond, and South can take his king.

South still wins only one diamond trick. The only difference is that he wins it with his own king instead of with dummy's jack. He therefore gets to dummy only once and can take only one club finesse. Down one instead of making game and rubber.

16. SAVE ENTRY FOR THE RIGHT TIME

Some players take pride in making the first play from dummy without the slightest delay. No prize is awarded for this sort of speed.

South dealer
North-South vulnerable

NORTH
♠ Q J 6
♡ 9 4 2
◇ K Q J 10 7
♣ 7 4

WEST
♠ 9 7 5 2
♡ 8 5
◇ 8 4 2
♣ K Q 10 3

EAST
♠ K 10 8
♡ J 10 7 3
◇ A 9 6 3
♣ 8 6

SOUTH
♠ A 4 3
♡ A K Q 6
◇ 5
♣ A J 9 5 2

South	West	North	East
1 ♣	Pass	1 ◇	Pass
1 ♡	Pass	2 ◇	Pass
3 NT	All Pass		

Opening lead — ♠ 2

West led the deuce of spades, and dummy made the mistake of putting his spades down before he put the other suits on the table. Quick as a flash, declarer played the queen of spades from dummy.

East was not in such a hurry. He waited to see the rest of the dummy before he made his first play. Then he carefully played the eight of spades, resisting the temptation to cover with the king.

Declarer next finessed the nine of clubs, losing to West's ten. West returned another spade, and this time East used the king to cover dummy's picture card.

South floundered about from here on, and eventually went down two. He could never bring in dummy's long diamonds, and nothing else broke well.

Less Haste

South took a long time about his floundering. He agonized over several unimportant plays late in the hand, hoping that something good would develop. If he had made his *first* play with less haste, he could have played the rest of the hand with more speed.

If you look at the *whole* dummy, you can see that dummy's long diamond suit will provide enough tricks—if you can reach them. The only sure side entry is in spades. For this reason, South must be sure to keep dummy's spade entry.

South should play a *low* spade from dummy at the first trick, and should win with the ace in his own hand. Then he leads diamonds until the ace is forced out.

Declarer can later lead a spade to force out the king, after which he can get to dummy by way of the last spade. This assures him of two spades, three hearts, four diamonds, and one club—more than enough tricks for the contract.

17. SAFETY PLAY ASSURES CONTRACT

How would you play the diamonds in this hand? Cover up the East-West cards and try to come up with the expert answer.

South dealer
North-South vulnerable

NORTH
♠ 6 5 4
♡ A K J
♦ A 9 5 3
♣ A Q 7

WEST	EAST
♠ 10 8 7	♠ K 9 3 2
♡ 7 4	♡ 9 8 6 5 3
♦ Q 10 8 2	♦ 7
♣ J 10 9 8	♣ 6 3 2

SOUTH
♠ A Q J
♡ Q 10 2
♦ K J 6 4
♣ K 5 4

South	West	North	East
1 NT	Pass	6 NT	All Pass

Opening lead — ♣ J

Strangely enough, you cannot answer the question until you have tested the spades. The correct play is to win the first club trick in dummy and immediately lead a spade to finesse the queen.

If this finesse wins, you can afford to lose one diamond trick. If the spade finesse loses, however, you must develop the diamonds without loss.

Suppose, first, that the spade finesse loses. Then you must go after all of the diamonds by leading a low diamond to the ace and then finessing the jack of diamonds. You must find Q-x or Q-x-x of diamonds in the East hand.

Safety Play Needed

If the spade finesse works, however, a safety play in diamonds is needed. You need only three diamond tricks.

Take the first diamond trick with the king and then lead a low diamond toward dummy.

If West plays a low diamond, you finesse dummy's nine. You won't mind losing that trick because the suit will break well if both opponents follow suit twice. As the cards lie, dummy's nine would win the trick, and your slam would be safe.

If West plays the ten or queen of diamonds, you can win with dummy's ace and lead the nine of diamonds back to set up the jack. This is very weak defense.

What happens if *West* has the singleton and East has four diamonds? In this case, West shows out when you lead the second diamond. This locates the rest of the diamonds for you. It's easy to go up with dummy's ace and return a diamond toward your jack.

In short, you are sure to make three diamond tricks by this method.

One of the exciting things about contract bridge is that you have the chance to pile up 50 points on a very strong hand. This isn't as good as piling up 800 points, but it keeps your partner from falling asleep.

South dealer
North-South vulnerable

NORTH
♠ Q 6 5
♡ 7 6 2
◇ 8 7 4 3
♣ J 7 3

WEST
♠ J 8 7 2
♡ K J 8 5 3
◇ 6 2
♣ K 8

EAST
♠ 10 9 4 3
♡ Q 9
◇ 10 9 5
♣ 10 9 5 4

SOUTH
♠ A K
♡ A 10 4
◇ A K Q J
♣ A Q 6 2

South	West	North	East
3 NT	All Pass		

Opening lead — ♡ 5

West opened the five of hearts, and East played the queen. South looked fondly at his magnificent hand and graciously conceded the first trick to East.

East returned a heart, and South won with the ace.

Declarer next ran his four top diamonds and the two top

spades. South then slyly led a low club toward dummy, perhaps hoping that West would be foolish enough to play low.

West sat up suddenly, like a man who had been reprieved—as was actually the case. He took the king of clubs and three more heart tricks, defeating the contract.

"Very sporting, old boy!" West said to declarer. And this was probably the only kind word that could be found for South's method of playing the hand.

Heart Lead Would Win

South had played the hand properly up to the time he led the low club. At that stage, however, he should have led his last heart.

West would take three heart tricks, but then he would have to lead a spade or a club. A spade lead would give a trick to dummy's queen; and a club lead would give South a free finesse. Either way, declarer would surely make his ninth trick.

Are you wondering how South managed to pile up 50 points on this hand? He had 150 honors, and thus came out with a 50-point profit in spite of his careless play. The opponents were willing to give him 50 points whenever he had that good a hand!

19. FREE FINESSE IS BEST

Once upon a time there was a poor but honest bridge player whose fairy godmother had given him a lucky coin. "When you don't know what to play," his godmother had told our hero, "toss the coin. Decide in advance that heads mean one play and that tails means the other play. The coin will always tell you what to do."

This worked very well for a year and a day, until along came this hand:

South dealer
North-South vulnerable

```
              NORTH
              ♠ A K 7 4
              ♡ 9 7 5
              ◇ A 3 2
              ♣ 8 6 3
WEST                      EAST
♠ 10 6                    ♠ J 9 8 5
♡ K 4 3                   ♡ J 10 8 6 2
◇ Q 10 8 6                ◇ 9 7
♣ K 10 7 4                ♣ J 9
              SOUTH
              ♠ Q 3 2
              ♡ A Q
              ◇ K J 5 4
              ♣ A Q 5 2
```

South	West	North	East
1 NT	Pass	3 NT	All Pass

Opening lead — ♣ 4

West opened the four of clubs, and our hero won with the queen. He took the three top spades, but the suit failed to break. West discarded a heart on the third spade.

Declarer counted eight tricks in top cards and saw that a successful finesse in either hearts or diamonds would give him his ninth trick. Which finesse to take?

He took the magic coin out of his pocket, decided to let hearts be heads and diamonds tails, and tossed the coin up to the ceiling. As the coin came down, West waited with a cynical look on his face. He didn't believe in magic, and besides he knew that both finesses were going to lose.

Coin Is Lost

The coin bounced out of the window and rolled down a nearby sewer. A great loss to South and also to the scientists at Duke University, who were planning to test the coin.

Fortunately our hero knew what to make of this unexpected accident. "This must be a warning not to take either finesse," he decided.

And he was quite right. Instead, he took the ace of clubs and led another club to let West take his tricks. This taught West not to be so cynical, for after he had taken two clubs he had to lead hearts or diamonds, and either lead would give South a free finesse for his ninth trick.

20. AN EASY SQUEEZE

If you stumble into a very fine play by accident just look superior, as though you had planned it all.

South dealer
North-South vulnerable

NORTH
♠ K J 10 7
♡ K 7 2
◇ 8 4 2
♣ J 10 6

WEST
♠ 8 4 3
♡ J 10 4
◇ J 9 5 3
♣ K 7 2

EAST
♠ 9 6 5 2
♡ A Q 9 8
◇ 7 6
♣ 9 5 4

SOUTH
♠ A Q
♡ 6 5 3
◇ A K Q 10
♣ A Q 8 3

South	West	North	East
1 ◇	Pass	1 ♠	Pass
2 NT	Pass	3 NT	All Pass

Opening lead — ♡ J

South should not have bid two notrump with the hearts wide open. As things worked out, his poor bid gave him the chance to execute a Vienna Coup.

The Vienna Coup, for the benefit of those who came in late, is a spectacular play in which you set up a high card for an opponent and then squeeze him out of it. In the days of whist the best players struggled for several days to work out such a play.

And now back to our hero. He lost the first four heart tricks, which served him right. On the fourth heart he discarded a diamond from the dummy and a club from his own hand.

West discarded the seven of clubs on the fourth heart, and East then led the nine of clubs. South wasn't the best player in the world, but he did know his playmates. West was incapable of signalling with the seven of clubs unless he had a high club.

Declines Finesse

South therefore declined the finesse. He put up the ace of clubs and ran the four spades, discarding the last two clubs from his hand. This left him with the four diamonds. South wasn't trying to do anything difficult. He just hoped that his four diamonds would all turn out to be good.

On the last spade West had to come down to four cards. He had the king of clubs and four diamonds to the jack. What could he discard? Dummy had the jack of clubs, and South had just discarded the queen of clubs.

So West discarded a diamond, and South thereupon took four diamond tricks. West had been squeezed out of his diamond stopper.

North, a fine player, had been watching with great excitement. "Marvelous," he exclaimed at the end of the hand. "A Vienna Coup!"

"Think nothing of it," South demurred modestly. "It was easy."

TRUMP HANDS

Most players get the feeling that the average notrump hand is more difficult than the average trump hand. The chief reason for this feeling is that a strong trump suit protects you from all harm; you don't have that kind of protection in a notrump hand.

When you do have a problem in a trump hand, however, it may well be tougher than anything you get in a notrump hand. The reason is that any notrump play may be made even when there is a trump suit; but you may, in addition, have trumping plays that cannot possibly occur in a notrump hand.

The Cross-Ruff

In No. 21, for example, we see an example of the cross-ruff. If the hand were played at notrump, South would be able to get only three spade tricks. When spades are trumps, however, South can try for seven or eight spade tricks.

There are some additional points to remember about cross-ruffing. For one thing, declarer cannot afford to draw trumps; every round of trumps may cost him a ruffing trick. A second point, illustrated in No. 21, is that declarer must cash his top cards in the side suits before proceeding with the cross-ruff.

A third point, the danger of an over-ruff, is dealt with in No. 22. When you must ruff

several times, it is usually wise to ruff first with low trumps since an early over-ruff is unlikely. Later, when the danger of an over-ruff is greater, you do your ruffing with high trumps. When safety permits, as in No. 22, you do most of the ruffing with high trumps.

Protecting Your Trumps

Unless you're lucky enough to have an overwhelmingly powerful trump suit you must nurse your trumps along to protect them against bad breaks, over-ruffs, and other diseases.

One simple way to protect yourself is to lead through an opponent's ace toward your own high cards. This permits you to save your high card when the opponent plays his ace. As we see in No. 23, the high card that you save may be the difference between a plus and a minus score.

Another way to maintain your trump length is to refuse to ruff. Discard a loser, as in No. 24, and keep all of your trumps. This type of play is especially important when you have only a 4-card trump suit.

When possible, save a trump in dummy to stop the enemy's long suit. This permits you to save all of your own trumps for the important job of drawing trumps and maintaining control of the hand. Hand No. 25 shows that it is sometimes necessary to tackle a side suit before drawing trumps, thus leaving a trump in dummy to act as a shield against the opponents.

Even when dummy's trumps cannot be used to protect you against the enemy's long suit, it may still pay you to postpone a ruff. The idea is to ruff when one of the opponents plays his last card of the dangerous long suit. If that opponent wins a trick, later, he will be unable to continue the dangerous suit. In effect, as we see in No. 26, you are executing a hold-up play—but with a trump instead of the more usual ace or king of the long suit.

The most remarkable hand in this series is No. 27, in which you must deliberately set up an opponent's trump by overtaking dummy's high trump with your own ace. Only in this way can you be in your own hand to lead a good side suit and stay one trump ahead of the opponent. If you stay in dummy, you'll have to waste a trump to get to your hand, and then you fall one trump behind the opponent.

Card-Reading

The biggest difference between the expert and the average player is that the expert is constantly trying to locate the cards that he cannot see in his own hand and the dummy. This is true whether he is playing the hand as declarer or whether he is defending.

The bidding furnishes the first clues to the location of the missing cards. When a player bids, you credit him with reasonable strength for his bid, together with length in the suit he has bid—or, in the case of a notrump bid, with balanced distribution.

What a player *fails* to do may tell you just as much as what he does do. In Hand No. 32, neither defender ever bids, but the failure to bid tells the story.

When the bidding doesn't tell the full story, you must call on the play of the cards to furnish extra evidence. Try to postpone a guess until you have piled up as many facts and clues as possible.

In No. 33, for example, you put off a guess in hearts until you have done some work on the clubs. By that time you know how to make the right guess.

The ability to count up to 13 in each suit is part of the expert's stock in trade. As you play the hand, you build up a little picture of each opponent's original hand. Eventually you know exactly how many cards each opponent holds in each suit. This information is often all you need to get the most out of the cards.

This type of counting is shown in No. 34 and No. 35. A player who has never taken the trouble to count will find it fatiguing at first but will develop stamina with practice. In a short time it becomes purely automatic—and more rewarding than anything else.

21. TAKE SIDE CARDS BEFORE CROSS-RUFFING

If a trick won't wait, take it while it's still good.

South dealer
East-West vulnerable

NORTH
- ♠ 10 9 8 6
- ♡ None
- ♢ A 8 7 3 2
- ♣ K 9 6 3

WEST
- ♠ None
- ♡ A J 8 3
- ♢ J 10 9 6 4
- ♣ Q 10 7 2

EAST
- ♠ A 5 4 3 2
- ♡ Q 9 6 5
- ♢ K 5
- ♣ J 8

SOUTH
- ♠ K Q J 7
- ♡ K 10 7 4 2
- ♢ Q
- ♣ A 5 4

South	West	North	East
1 ♠	Pass	4 ♠	Pass
Pass	Pass		

Opening lead — ◇ J

West opened the jack of diamonds, and declarer won with dummy's ace. So far, so good.

South saw that he would have to rely on a cross-ruff. That is, he would ruff diamonds in his own hand and hearts in the dummy. This was a correct analysis, but he forgot one important point.

At the second trick, South ruffed a diamond in his hand. He ruffed a heart in dummy and led another diamond from dummy. East discarded a club, and South ruffed.

South had already lost his contract, but he persisted in his error. He ruffed another heart in dummy and led another diamond. East discarded his other club, thus making sure that South would never get a club trick.

South ruffed and led a third heart, ruffing in dummy. He led dummy's last diamond, and East stepped up with the ace of trumps and led another trump. South had taken eight tricks by this time, but he couldn't take any more. Down two.

Overlooks Principle

South had overlooked a fundamental principle of cross-ruffing. You must cash high cards in the side suits before you start the cross-ruff.

The correct line of play is to win the first trick with the ace of diamonds, and then to take the king and ace of clubs. Those tricks are good early but won't remain good much longer, as South found out.

Having taken his club tricks, South can cross-ruff. He will then make the ten tricks needed for his game contract.

22. DON'T SEND A BOY

According to the latest statistics, 119 times each hour some declarer ruffs with a low trump and thus allows an opponent to over-ruff. In 115 of these cases, the opponent remarks: "Don't send a boy to do a man's job."

South dealer
North-South vulnerable

```
                NORTH
                ♠ Q J 8 3
                ♡ A Q 6 4 2
                ◇ J
                ♣ J 6 3
WEST                      EAST
♠ 10 6 2                  ♠ 7 5
♡ 9 5                     ♡ K J 10 8 3
◇ Q 10 6 5 2             ◇ 8 4
♣ 8 4 2                   ♣ Q 10 9 7
                SOUTH
                ♠ A K 9 4
                ♡ 7
                ◇ A K 9 7 3
                ♣ A K 5
```

South	West	North	East
1 ◇	Pass	1 ♡	Pass
2 ♠	Pass	4 ♠	Pass
4 NT	Pass	5 ◇	Pass
5 NT	Pass	6 ♣	Pass
6 ♠	All Pass		

Opening lead — ♡ 9

Declarer quite properly began by cashing his five top cards in the side suits. He discarded a club from dummy, ruffed a club in dummy, ruffed a heart in his own hand, ruffed a diamond in dummy, and ruffed another heart in his own hand.

Unfortunately for South, he ruffed the heart with the nine of spades. West over-ruffed with the ten of spades, making the time-honored remark about men and boys. Then West returned another trump.

This was the end for South. He still had two losing diamonds, and dummy had only one trump. Down one.

Slam Is Cold

The slam is actually cold after South has managed to ruff once in each hand with a low trump. The right line of play is to send four men to do a boy's job.

At this stage South has A-K-9 of trumps and three low diamonds. Dummy has Q-J-8 of trumps and three low hearts. It is no longer safe to ruff with low trumps.

South should lead a diamond and ruff with dummy's jack. He returns a heart and ruffs with the king. He leads another diamond, ruffing with dummy's queen. He next ruffs a heart with the ace. He can then lead his last diamond and ruff with dummy's eight.

One of the opponents can take the ten of trumps at the twelfth or thirteenth trick, but South cannot be defeated.

One way to promote your minor honors is to capture an opponent's high card. The opponent must be on the alert to prevent this.

East dealer
Both sides vulnerable

NORTH
♠ J 5 3
♡ 6 5 3 2
♢ K Q J 7
♣ A Q

WEST
♠ 10 9 4
♡ 10 7
♢ 8 5 2
♣ 9 6 5 4 2

EAST
♠ A 6
♡ K Q J 9 4
♢ 9 4 3
♣ K 8 3

SOUTH
♠ K Q 8 7 2
♡ A 8
♢ A 10 6
♣ J 10 7

East	South	West	North
1 ♡	1 ♠	Pass	3 ♠
Pass	4 ♠	All Pass	

Opening lead — ♡ 10

South won the first heart with the ace and led a low trump toward dummy. East captured dummy's jack with the ace—an important step in promoting a trump trick for his partner.

East then continued hearts. On the third round of hearts, South was in the middle. If he ruffed with the king or queen, West's ten of trumps would later become established. If South ruffed low, West would over-ruff immediately. Either way, South was sure to go down.

Avoid Capture

South can make his contract by avoiding the capture of a trump honor. It is clear that East has the ace of spades (for his opening bid), so declarer must lead low trumps through East.

On winning the first trick, South leads a diamond to dummy and returns a low trump. East's best play is to duck, and South wins with the king.

South leads another diamond to dummy and returns another low spade. East plays the ace, and South is able to play a low card. East has captured nothing but small cards with his ace.

East can now lead hearts through South, but South can ruff the third round of hearts with the queen of spades. This shuts out West's ten. Then declarer leads a trump to dummy's jack to pick up West's last trump. The rest is easy.

All of the textbooks advise you to look for a trump suit in which you and dummy have a combined length of eight cards. This is excellent advice, but what are you supposed to do when no such suit exists?

West dealer
North-South vulnerable

NORTH
♠ J 7 3
♡ A 4 3
♢ 8 7 3
♣ A K 8 4

WEST
♠ 10 9 6 4
♡ 10 9 7 6
♢ 10 2
♣ Q 10 5

EAST
♠ 8 2
♡ 8 5
♢ A K Q 9 5 4
♣ J 6 3

SOUTH
♠ A K Q 5
♡ K Q J 2
♢ J 6
♣ 9 7 2

West	North	East	South
Pass	1 ♣	3 ♢	3 ♡
Pass	4 ♡	All Pass	

Opening lead — ♢ 10

Spades and hearts were both reasonable trump suits. When you can't find a suit with eight cards, it's quite all right to settle for a 4-3 fit—especially if your suit is headed by most or all of the top cards.

When your trump suit is short, however, you must handle it with care. One untimely ruff may cost you the contract.

In this case South fell from grace. West opened the ten of diamonds, and East led out his three top cards. South made the fatal error of ruffing the third diamond with a high trump.

West discarded a spade on the third diamond. Now South hopefully led out three rounds of trumps. This left West with a good trump. West eventually made his trump and a club trick, defeating the contract.

Should Discard

When the third diamond is led, South should discard a low club. No matter how the hand develops South is sure to lose this club trick sooner or later. It costs nothing to give the trick up at this moment and save all of the trumps for more important work.

East cannot afford to lead another diamond, for then *dummy* will ruff. If East leads anything else, declarer can win and draw four rounds of trumps. South easily wins four trumps, four spades, and two clubs, making his contract.

Do you feel ashamed when you put down a singleton deuce of trumps in the dummy? You can't help feeling that your partner might have picked a better suit, but don't despair; your deuce may yet save the day.

West dealer
Both sides vulnerable

NORTH
♠ 8 7 6 4 3 2
♡ 2
◇ Q J 9 2
♣ 8 4

WEST
♠ A 9
♡ 10 9 7 4
◇ 8 3
♣ A K J 7 2

EAST
♠ J 10 5
♡ 8 6
◇ A 7 6
♣ Q 10 9 5 3

SOUTH
♠ K Q
♡ A K Q J 5 3
◇ K 10 5 4
♣ 6

West	North	East	South
1 ♣	Pass	2 ♣	4 ♡
All Pass			

Opening lead — ♣ K

West opens the king of clubs and continues with the ace. South must ruff since he must still lose a spade and a diamond. He cannot afford to give up two club tricks.

What should South do next? If South draws trumps, he must use four trumps for the purpose. This will leave him with only one trump. He knocks out the ace of diamonds, and back comes a club, forcing out his last trump.

West saves the ace of spades and a club to win the last two tricks, and South is down one.

Trumps Must Wait

What about that deuce we were discussing? If you allow it to stay in dummy, the deuce of trumps will prevent the opponents from leading a third club.

Instead of drawing trumps immediately, you must first knock out an ace. Which ace?

Not diamonds. If you lead diamonds before drawing trumps, somebody will get a diamond ruff.

Lead the queen of spades. With luck, you may sneak the trick by. If so, you will immediately switch to four rounds of trumps.

Even if West takes the queen of spades with his ace, he can do no damage. He cannot lead a third club, since dummy's deuce of trumps stands guard to protect the trumps in the South hand. If West leads anything else, you regain the lead, draw four rounds of trumps and concede the ace of diamonds.

26. HOLD UP A TRUMP

You've often held up an ace to cut communications between the opponents, but have you ever withheld a trump for the same reason? It's a play you should get to know.

South dealer
North-South vulnerable

NORTH
♠ 8 7 2
♡ Q 8 4
◇ 8 5 4
♣ K 6 3 2

WEST
♠ A K 5 3
♡ 7 3
◇ Q 9 2
♣ Q J 10 7

EAST
♠ 4
♡ 9 6 5 2
◇ A K J 10 6 3
♣ 9 8

SOUTH
♠ Q J 10 9 6
♡ A K J 10
◇ 7
♣ A 5 4

South	West	North	East
1 ♠	Pass	1 NT	2 ◇
2 ♡	3 ◇	Pass	Pass
3 ♠	All Pass		

Opening lead — ◇ 2

West leads the deuce of diamonds, and East wins with the king. East continues with the ace of diamonds and South has a key play to make.

If South ruffs, he is a peeled potato. West unblocks with the queen of diamonds, of course. South must lead a trump, and West wisely refuses the first trump trick.

South must lead another trump, and this time West takes the ace and king of spades. This draws dummy's trumps and leaves one trump in the West and one trump in the South hand. Now West leads his last diamond.

If South ruffs, he will be out of trumps. West will surely get a trump trick and a club to defeat the contract. If South fails to ruff the third round of diamonds, East will just continue diamonds until South does ruff. The contract is doomed.

Must Not Ruff

South can make the contract by refusing to ruff a diamond at the second trick. Instead, he discards the low club that he is sure to lose in any case. Diamonds are continued, and this time South ruffs.

Notice the effect. West is now out of diamonds. Whenever West wins a trump trick he cannot lead another diamond to renew the attack on South's trumps. It doesn't matter whether West shifts to clubs or to hearts: South can draw all of the trumps and make his contract.

This is just the same play you make at notrump when you hold up an ace until one opponent plays his last card of the suit. Your trump takes the place of the ace.

[43]

My father taught me the facts of life. "Son," he said, "you're old enough now to know the truth. Your opponents aren't going to help you. They're out for themselves, drat 'em." He was right, too.

North dealer
Both sides vulnerable

NORTH
♠ A
♡ K Q J
♢ A K Q 4
♣ 10 8 7 6 2

WEST
♠ 5
♡ 10 9 8 3
♢ 7 6
♣ A K Q J 9 5

EAST
♠ 9 7 6 4 3 2
♡ 6
♢ J 10 9 8
♣ 4 3

SOUTH
♠ K Q J 10 8
♡ A 7 5 4 2
♢ 5 3 2
♣ None

North	East	South	West
1 ♢	Pass	1 ♠	2 ♣
Double	Pass	3 ♡	Pass
6 ♡	All Pass		

Opening lead — ♣ K

West opened the king of clubs, and South ruffed. South led a trump to the king and continued with the queen of trumps. East discarded a spade, and South saw trouble ahead.

Declarer cashed dummy's ace of spades and then drew a third round of trumps with dummy's jack. This left South with just the ace of trumps, and West with just the ten.

Declarer now led out dummy's top diamonds. He reasoned that West would trump a diamond, using up his only trump for this purpose. This would leave South in control of the situation with the ace of trumps and good spades.

Nobody had told South the facts of life. West just refused to ruff the third diamond. West saw no reason to help South out of his pickle.

No Escape

Now there was no escape. Declarer had to lead a club or a diamond from dummy. He had to use up the ace of hearts, leaving West with the last trump and the rest of the clubs. Down three!

South should make the slam by careful play. He overtakes the jack of hearts with the ace. This leaves South in his own hand with a low trump and four good spades. West has the ten of trumps. South proceeds to lead out high spades until West trumps. Then South has control with the last trump and the rest of the spades.

It's unusual to overtake your own jack of trumps with the ace and thus establish the ten of trumps for an opponent. The advantage of being in the correct hand may make up for this unusual play. In this case, the right play would have made a difference of three tricks.

28. SET UP A SHORT SUIT

Some tricks lie on the surface. You pick them up without any effort. Other tricks lie deep beneath the ground. You need a pickaxe to get at them. Never mind; the exercise is good for you.

West dealer
Both sides vulnerable

NORTH
♠ 10 9 8
♡ J 10 9 3
♢ 8 5 3
♣ 9 3 2

WEST
♠ 6
♡ A K Q 6 2
♢ Q J 9
♣ Q J 8 5

EAST
♠ 7 4
♡ 8 7 5 4
♢ K 10 7 4
♣ K 10 7

SOUTH
♠ A K Q J 5 3 2
♡ None
♢ A 6 2
♣ A 6 4

West	North	East	South
1 ♡	Pass	2 ♡	4 ♠
All Pass			

Opening lead — ♡ K

Suppose you are the declarer in this hand. You need ten tricks for your contract. You can easily take seven trumps and two aces, for those nine tricks are right on the surface.

Where is the tenth trick?

It is quite clear that the tenth trick must be a heart since nothing else can possibly become a trick. If it isn't equally clear how you can win a heart trick, just spit on your hands and get the pickaxe ready.

Don't Draw Trumps

One thing to note is that you cannot afford to draw trumps. When you have established a heart trick, you will want to reach dummy to cash it. One of dummy's trumps will be the entry that permits you to reach dummy for that purpose.

Ruff the opening lead with a high trump. Lead a low trump to dummy's eight and return the jack of hearts.

East plays low, naturally enough, and you discard a low diamond. West wins with the queen of hearts and returns the queen of diamonds. You win with the ace of diamonds and lead a low trump to dummy's nine. You then lead the ten of hearts from dummy, discarding the last diamond from your hand.

West wins with the ace of hearts and leads another diamond. You ruff with a high spade and lead your last low spade to dummy's ten. This puts you in dummy and enables you to cash the nine of hearts—your vital tenth trick.

If you have two chances for your contract, which should you try for first?

South dealer
North-South vulnerable

NORTH
♠ J 3
♡ Q 10 8 7 6 2
◇ J 6
♣ 6 5 3

WEST
♠ A 8 7 5
♡ 3
◇ 9 7 5 2
♣ 10 9 8 7

EAST
♠ Q 10 9 4 2
♡ 4
◇ K 10 8 4 3
♣ 4 2

SOUTH
♠ K 6
♡ A K J 9 5
◇ A Q
♣ A K Q J

South	West	North	East
2 ♡	Pass	2 NT	Pass
3 ♣	Pass	4 ♡	Pass
6 ♡	All Pass		

Opening lead — ♣ 10

Imagine that you are South. How would you plan your play?

Naturally, you win the first trick and draw one round of trumps. No problem about that. But plan the later play. (As a matter of fact, you should make the full plan before touching the first card from the dummy.)

You can confidently expect to win six trumps, four clubs, and the ace of diamonds. You need one additional trick. Should you lead a spade toward the king, or should you lead a

diamond from dummy in order to finesse the queen?

If you are blessed with normal curiosity, you will already know that the spade try happens to fail and that the diamond finesse will work. Does this mean that you should try the diamond finesse and abandon the attempt to win a spade trick?

Not at all. If you were actually playing the hand you would not be able to see the defensive hands. Unless you have actually seen the king of diamonds in the East hand, you should try first for a spade trick.

Can You Recover?

In choosing the right suit to play first, the question to ask yourself is: "Can I recover if my guess is wrong?"

If you take the diamond finesse and happen to lose to the king, the defenders will take the ace of spades. Recovery will then be impossible.

Suppose that you draw a trump and run the four clubs, discarding a spade from dummy. Now enter dummy with a trump and lead dummy's only remaining spade. If you lose the king of spades, you are not yet beaten. You can still get back to dummy with a trump in order to try the diamond finesse.

In short, the spade play gives you both chances. The diamond play gives you only one chance. Half a loaf may be better than none, but the whole loaf is better still!

As we grow older we learn how to say things elegantly. For example, South claimed that he was the victim of an optical illusion in this hand. Very elegant. When South was a little boy, however, his mother used to tell him that his eyes were bigger than his stomach.

South dealer
North-South vulnerable

NORTH
♠ A Q J 9 3
♡ A 2
♢ J 7 4
♣ 10 7 3

WEST	EAST
♠ 8 5 4	♠ K 7 2
♡ 7 6 4	♡ 8
♢ 6 5 3	♢ Q 8 2
♣ 9 8 5 2	♣ A K Q J 6 4

SOUTH
♠ 10 6
♡ K Q J 10 9 5 3
♢ A K 10 9
♣ None

South	West	North	East
1 ♡	Pass	1 ♠	2 ♣
3 ♣	Pass	3 ♠	Pass
4 ♡	Pass	5 ♡	Pass
6 ♡	All Pass		

Opening lead — ♣ 2

West opened the deuce of clubs, and South ruffed. Declarer drew three rounds of trumps and then led the ten of spades for a finesse.

The hand looked fairly simple. South needed either the spade finesse or the diamond finesse to make his slam. At least that's the way it appeared.

When South led the ten of spades for a finesse, East casually played low. This was, of course, the best defense. If East took the first spade trick, the rest of dummy's spades would give South all the discards he needed.

South thought that this trick settled his choice between the spade and diamond finesses. "A bird in the hand," he muttered, "is worth two in the bush." After corning this phrase, South led his other spade and finessed dummy's jack.

East pounced on this trick with the king of spades and returned a club. Now South might huff and puff, but he still had to lose a diamond trick for down one.

South Was Greedy

South was just greedy when he took the second spade finesse. After the 10 of spades won, South could make sure of the slam by taking the ace of spades and getting to work on the diamonds. If the diamond finesse worked, he would make an extra trick, but his slam was safe even if the diamond finesse should lose.

When a hand looks difficult from your side of the table, imagine that you are on the other side of the table. It may be no problem at all when you change your point of view.

South dealer
Neither side vulnerable

NORTH
♠ A Q 9 8 4
♡ K J 9
♢ A 7
♣ A Q 5

WEST	EAST
♠ 5 2	♠ K J 10 6 3
♡ 4 2	♡ 6 5 3
♢ K J 6 3 2	♢ 10 9 8
♣ 7 6 3 2	♣ 9 8

SOUTH
♠ 7
♡ A Q 10 8 7
♢ Q 5 4
♣ K J 10 4

South	West	North	East
1 ♡	Pass	2 ♠	Pass
3 ♡	Pass	4 NT	Pass
5 ♢	Pass	5 NT	Pass
6 ♢	Pass	7 ♡	Pass
Pass	Pass		

Opening lead — ♠ 5

West opened the five of spades, and South wondered what to do about the losing diamonds. He thought of drawing just one round of trumps and then running all four clubs. This would allow him to discard the losing diamond from dummy if either opponent had four trumps and also four or more clubs.

Very unlikely, South decided. The situation looked hopeless, until he thought of playing the hand as though North were declarer. North would ruff out the losing spades, so South proceeded with that plan.

He won the first trick with the ace of spades and ruffed a spade. He returned to dummy with the queen of clubs to ruff a second spade. He got back with the ace of clubs to ruff a third spade, and led to the ace of diamonds to ruff the last spade with the ace of trumps.

One Trump Left

Having ruffed four times, South had only one trump left in his hand: the queen. He led this and overtook with dummy's king of hearts. He proceeded to lead out the jack and nine of hearts from dummy, discarding two diamonds from his own hand. The king and jack of clubs then took the last two tricks.

Did you foresee that South would discard his losing diamonds on dummy's trumps?

32. WHAT DIDN'T HAPPEN?

Every bridge player should know the Sherlock Holmes story of the dog that barked in the night. You see, the dog didn't bark. And this was the whole point of the case.

Wondering how we can get barking dogs mixed up with a bridge hand? Stay with us.

East dealer
North-South vulnerable

NORTH
♠ J 10 9 4
♡ A J 3
♢ Q 7 4
♣ A 5 4

WEST
♠ 6 3
♡ Q 8 6
♢ J 10 9 5
♣ 9 6 3 2

EAST
♠ Q 5
♡ 9 7 4 2
♢ A K 6 2
♣ K 8 7

SOUTH
♠ A K 8 7 2
♡ K 10 5
♢ 8 3
♣ Q J 10

East	South	West	North
Pass	1 ♠	Pass	3 ♠
Pass	4 ♠	Pass	Pass
Pass			

Opening lead — ♢ J

West opened the jack of diamonds, and South played low from dummy. West continued with the ten of diamonds, and declarer put up the queen from dummy. East took the king of diamonds and led the ace, forcing declarer to ruff.

No dog so far.

South led out the ace and king of spades, dropping the queen. Business was picking up. He then led the queen of clubs for a finesse, losing to the king.

Right here, South thought of the dog that hadn't barked.

East had already played the ace and king of diamonds, the queen of spades, and the king of clubs. Yet East had failed to open the bidding! Here was the dog that hadn't barked.

Locates Queen

This was important to South because his contract now depended on how he finessed for the queen of hearts. He could lead a heart from his hand to finesse dummy's jack, or he could lead a heart from dummy to finesse his own ten. He couldn't afford to guess wrong.

South no longer had to guess. Like Sherlock Holmes, he knew. East couldn't hold the queen of hearts, for then he would have opened the bidding. He had already shown up with 12 points in high cards, and couldn't have another 2 points in view of his original pass.

So South won the club return (after East took the king of clubs) and confidently finessed through West for the queen of hearts.

33. THE INDIRECT METHOD

People don't always answer direct questions. Ask a man how much money he has in his pocket, and he'll probably give you a rude answer. But you might well find out by some indirect way, such as asking to compare serial numbers on his paper money and dates on his coins. This kind of devious approach is necessary on some bridge hands.

West dealer
Both sides vulnerable

NORTH
♠ K 10 9 6
♡ K J 8
◇ 8 7 6 4
♣ 10 5

WEST	EAST
♠ 7 2	♠ 3
♡ A 4 3	♡ Q 10 6 5 2
◇ A K J 9 5	◇ 10 3 2
♣ 9 8 2	♣ A J 7 4

SOUTH
♠ A Q J 8 5 4
♡ 9 7
◇ Q
♣ K Q 6 3

West	North	East	South
1 ◇	Pass	1 ♡	1 ♠
Pass	2 ♠	Pass	4 ♠
All Pass			

Opening lead — ◇ K

In this hand South wants to know who has the ace of hearts. But if he asks the direct question, nobody will tell him.

West leads the king of diamonds and continues with the ace, and South ruffs. A naive declarer would draw trumps and lead a heart toward dummy. "Have the tooth out," he would say to himself.

West would play a low heart, giving South his chance to guess. And now South has to wonder who has the ace of hearts. If West has the ace, declarer should play the king of hearts from dummy; but if East has the ace, South's only chance is to finesse dummy's jack of hearts.

Our naive declarer will sometimes guess right, but just as often he will guess wrong.

Sidelong Approach

The way to find out about the ace of hearts may come from playing the clubs. It's devious, but very logical.

West is known to have a good diamond suit, but he needs a side ace to justify his vulnerable opening bid. He may have the ace of hearts or the ace of clubs. You don't know which.

After ruffing the second diamond, lead a trump to dummy and return a club. East may play low, and you will win with the king. Lead another trump to dummy, and return another club. This time East must put up the ace of clubs.

Now you know that West doesn't have the ace of clubs. Therefore he must have the ace of hearts. And this information tells you how to make your contract.

Scientists have discovered that certain birds are able to count up to four but not up to five. How on earth do those birds wind up so often as my bridge partners? Let scientists answer *that* question.

South dealer
East-West vulnerable

NORTH
♠ A K 7 3
♡ 9 3
◇ J 10 8 3
♣ K 10 6

WEST
♠ Q 8 5 4
♡ A K J 8 7 2
◇ 7 2
♣ 8

EAST
♠ J 10 6 2
♡ Q 4
◇ 9 4
♣ Q 9 5 4 2

SOUTH
♠ 9
♡ 10 6 5
◇ A K Q 6 5
♣ A J 7 3

South	West	North	East
1 ◇	1 ♡	1 ♠	Pass
2 ♣	Pass	3 ◇	Pass
4 ◇	Pass	5 ◇	All Pass

Opening lead — ♡ K

West opened the king of hearts, continued with the ace of hearts, and then led the jack of hearts. My fine feathered friend ruffed high in the dummy, and East discarded a low club.

South drew two rounds of trumps, cashed the ace of clubs, and then led a club toward dummy. West discarded a heart, and South began to twitter and flutter. It was a pretty sight, but it had no effect on our hard-hearted opponents. East was sure to get a club trick, and South was down one.

Now let's see what counting has to do with all this.

South ruffs the third heart and draws one round of trumps. Well and good. Now he takes the top spades, ruffs a spade with a high trump, gets to dummy with the jack of diamonds (drawing the trumps in the process), and ruffs dummy's last spade.

Still Needs Finesse

South still needs the club finesse to make his contract. The difference is that he need not guess how to take it.

East could follow to only two hearts and only two diamonds. Each opponent had exactly four spades. This accounts for only eight of East's 13 cards. The other five cards simply have to be clubs.

South knows that East has five of the missing six clubs. It is therefore quite safe to draw West's singleton club with dummy's king and then lead through East for a finesse.

To discover how to play one suit you may have to get evidence from another suit.

West dealer
North-South vulnerable

NORTH
♠ 8 4 3
♡ 6 3
◇ 8 5 3 2
♣ A J 6 4

WEST
♠ K Q J 10 7
♡ 4
◇ K Q J 10 9
♣ 3 2

EAST
♠ 9 5 2
♡ J 7 5 2
◇ 7 4
♣ Q 10 9 8

SOUTH
♠ A 6
♡ A K Q 10 9 8
◇ A 6
♣ K 7 5

West	North	East	South
1 ♠	Pass	Pass	Double
2 ◇	Pass	2 ♠	3 ♡
Pass	4 ♡	All Pass	

Opening lead — ♠ K

West opens the king of spades, and you win with the ace. You see fairly quickly that your contract depends on avoiding the loss of a trump trick.

How do you play the trumps? Do you lead out the top cards in the hope of dropping the jack? Or do you finesse through East on the theory that he has four trumps headed by the jack?

Every reader of this column can see the correct answer. At the bridge table, however, the opponents wouldn't show you their cards. How would you know what to do?

Consider Bidding

You can get a valuable clue if you consider the bidding. West should have ten cards in spades and diamonds combined. Therefore he should have only three cards in clubs and hearts combined.

If you want to find out about West's hearts, set to work on his clubs and you'll get the answer.

At the second trick lead out the ace of hearts. If the jack drops you won't have to worry about the rest of the hand. As it happens, the jack doesn't fall.

Next cash the king of clubs. This is a slight risk, but well worth taking. When West follows suit, lead another club.

You're not afraid of a singleton club in the West hand. If West ruffs the second club you can play low from dummy, saving the ace for later use.

When West shows up with a second club, you know what to do about the trumps. You have already seen West play a heart and two clubs. This accounts for his three cards in those two suits. You can confidently lead a heart from dummy in order to finesse the ten from your hand.

Correct play of a key suit may be difficult even when you can see all of the missing cards.

```
        South dealer
     East-West vulnerable
           NORTH
          ♠ J 10 4
          ♡ A 7 4
          ◇ 5 4 3
          ♣ K 7 6 5
WEST                    EAST
♠ K 9 7                 ♠ 6
♡ K J 3                 ♡ 10 5
◇ Q J 10                ◇ A 9 8 7 6
♣ A Q 4 2               ♣ J 10 9 8 3
           SOUTH
          ♠ A Q 8 5 3 2
          ♡ Q 9 8 6 2
          ◇ K 2
          ♣ None
```

South	West	North	East
1 ♠	1 NT	2 ♠	3 ◇
3 ♡	Pass	3 ♠	4 ♣
4 ♠	Pass	Pass	Pass

Opening lead — ◇ Q

When the hand was actually played, South could see only his own hand and the dummy. However, West's vulnerable overcall of one notrump indicated a holding of 16 to 18 points in high cards. This was enough to tell South what he needed to know.

West opened the queen of dia-monds, and East won with the ace. East returned a trump, and South finessed to the king. West returned a trump, and dummy won with the ten. Now it was up to South to pull a rabbit out of the hat in the play of the hearts.

South led a low heart from dummy. East played low, and declarer finessed the eight, los-ing to the jack.

West returned a trump, and South won with the ace. Now South led the queen of hearts, and the defenders could get no further heart tricks. West's king was trapped, and East's ten of hearts was picked up on the same trick.

Other Plays Fail

It's worth noting that other plays would fail to limit the de-fenders to one heart trick.

South gains nothing by lead-ing the queen of hearts first from his hand. West covers with the king to drive out dummy's ace. The ten and jack of hearts then win separately.

South likewise gains nothing by leading a low heart first from his hand. West plays low, and South is doomed to lose two tricks in the suit.

Every bridge player should become familiar with a group of plays known as "safety plays." Most of them cost nothing; they may save you from partner's curled lip.

South dealer
East-West vulnerable

NORTH
♠ 6 5
♡ 7 6 4 3
◇ Q 6 3
♣ 8 4 3 2

WEST
♠ 2
♡ A Q J 8
◇ 1 0 8 7 5
♣ Q J 1 0 6

EAST
♠ Q J 4 3
♡ K 1 0 9 2
◇ J 9 4
♣ 9 7

SOUTH
♠ A K 1 0 9 8 7
♡ 5
◇ A K 2
♣ A K 5

South	West	North	East
2 ♠	Pass	2 NT	Pass
3 ♠	Pass	3 NT	Pass
4 ♠	All Pass		

Opening lead — ♣ Q

West leads the queen of clubs, and South wins with the king. How should South proceed?

He expects to lose a club and a heart. His problem is to lose only one trump trick.

If West has Q-J-x-x of trumps, he will get his two trump tricks no matter how South sobs and

sighs. But if *East* has Q-J-x-x of trumps, there is no need for South to despair.

South begins by leading out the ace of trumps. If an honor drops, South can continue to lead trumps from his own hand.

Get to Dummy

When only small trumps drop, South must next get to dummy with the queen of diamonds. Then he leads dummy's remaining trump.

East shrewdly plays a low trump, hoping that South will put up the king. After all, East would gain nothing by playing the jack or queen of trumps; this would merely make things easier for South.

When East plays a low trump, South must finesse the ten. This finesse is a standard safety play.

If West can win the trick, only one trump will be left. South will regain the lead and draw the last trump. If West cannot win the trick, as in this case, the safety finesse is needed to make the contract.

This type of safety play is recommended in all cases except when the defenders are likely to get a ruffing trick. That danger would influence you to draw trumps as quickly as possible instead of taking a safety play.

How do you force the opponents to take the ace and king of trumps on the same trick? Hypnotism is one answer, but this hand shows an easier method.

West dealer
East-West vulnerable

NORTH
♠ 5
♡ J 8
◇ Q 8 6 4 2
♣ K Q 10 7 3

WEST
♠ K J
♡ K Q 9 4 2
◇ K 3
♣ J 8 6 2

EAST
♠ Q 7 4 3 2
♡ 7 6 5 3
◇ A 5
♣ 5 4

SOUTH
♠ A 10 9 8 6
♡ A 10
◇ J 10 9 7
♣ A 9

West	North	East	South
1 ♡	2 NT(!)	3 ♡	5 ◇
Double	Pass	Pass	Pass

Opening lead — ♡ K

North's bid of two notrump was the Unusual Notrump—a sort of takeout double, asking partner to bid a minor suit.

South jumped all the way to game, reasoning that he was expected to bid three of a minor with a very poor hand and was therefore entitled to bid game with three aces.

West opened the king of hearts, and South had to worry about a heart loser and two top trumps. Fortunately for him, he was a good worrier.

The first step was to take the ace of hearts and start the clubs. When the queen of clubs was led from dummy, East had to ruff to prevent South from discarding his losing heart. What's more, East had to ruff with his low trump, since South would cheerfully discard his losing heart if East ruffed with the ace of trumps.

South overruffed, cashed the ace of spades, and ruffed a spade in dummy. Then he led a low club from dummy and ruffed in his own hand. This set up dummy's last club.

How to get to the dummy? South led another spade. West didn't dare step up with the king of trumps, for then dummy would discard the losing heart. So West had to discard, and dummy ruffed.

Now declarer could lead the last club from dummy. East discarded, for it would do him no good to ruff with the ace of trumps. South finally got rid of his losing heart, and West ruffed with his low trump.

The Big Clash

This paved the way for the big clash. Both defenders had been forced to use up their low trumps. When South regained the lead, he could lead a trump —and the ace and king of trumps clashed on the same trick.

Some bridge hands are like the old movies. The villain may be laughing and stroking his big black mustache, but you just know that the hero will somehow escape. The only trouble is that you can't see how he can possibly do it.

East dealer
North-South vulnerable

NORTH
♠ A 4 3
♡ 9 5 4
◇ J 7 4 3
♣ 8 4 3

WEST
♠ K Q 5 2
♡ K 10 7 3 2
◇ Q 10 6 2
♣ None

EAST
♠ None
♡ Q J 6
◇ 9 8 5
♣ Q J 10 9 7 5 2

SOUTH
♠ J 10 9 8 7 6
♡ A 8
◇ A K
♣ A K 6

East	South	West	North
4 ♣	4 ♠	Double	All Pass

Opening lead — ♡ 3

You are the hero, playing the South hand. West leads a low heart, and East plays the jack. West laughs villainously.

What are you going to do about it? If you let East win a heart trick, he will return the queen of clubs. Terrible things will happen.

Don't give up. The U.S. Marines, or somebody, will come to your rescue. Or, if you prefer, you can rescue yourself.

Shut East Out

The important thing is to shut East out of the lead. If you let him win a trick, he will lead the queen of clubs and then you will be beyond the help of even the Marines.

How can you prevent East from ever winning a heart trick? Discard your low heart on a trick that only West can win.

Win the first trick with the ace of hearts. Cash both top diamonds. Lead the jack of spades toward dummy.

West covers with the queen, and you win in dummy with the ace. Return the jack of diamonds from dummy and discard your low heart on this trick. West must win with queen of diamonds and now cannot lead a heart to his partner's hand.

No matter what West does, you can force out the king of spades and draw trumps. After drawing trumps you can take your top clubs and give up the last trick to East's queen of clubs.

"Foiled again!" snarls the villain.

40. THE SMOTHER PLAY

It isn't easy to find the winning line of play in this hand even when you can see all of the cards. Try it.

East dealer
Both sides vulnerable

NORTH
♠ A 4 2
♡ J 7 3
◇ K 10 9
♣ K 10 9 7

WEST	EAST
♠ Q 7 6 5	♠ 3
♡ 9 6	♡ A K Q 10 5 4
◇ 6 5 3 2	◇ 8 7 4
♣ 5 3 2	♣ Q J 8

SOUTH
♠ K J 10 9 8
♡ 8 2
◇ A Q J
♣ A 6 4

East	South	West	North
1 ♡	1 ♠	Pass	2 ♠
Pass	4 ♠	Pass	Pass
Pass			

Opening lead — ♡ 9

West opened the nine of hearts, and East continued the suit. South had to ruff the third heart with the king of spades to shut out an over-ruff. West could discard a club or diamond, as he chose. It made no difference.

South next led the jack of spades for a finesse. West played low, of course, and the jack held the trick.

South continued with the ten of spades, and this also held the trick. East discarded a heart, and it looked as though South had to lose a trump and a club.

Proceed from here. Can you make the contract?

How can you pick up the guarded queen of trumps with dummy's blank ace? Strangely enough, it can be done.

Abandon Trumps

You abandon the trumps. You cash all of the diamonds and the top clubs. Then you give up a club trick to East.

By this time, dummy is reduced to the ace of trumps and a club. West and you have two trumps each. East has only two hearts.

East must lead a heart, and you play the eight or nine of spades. If West ruffs with the queen, you win with dummy's ace of trumps; and then your last trump is good. If West ruffs low, your eight or nine will hold the trick; and then dummy's ace of trumps will take the last trick.

Either way, you win both of those last two tricks.

Incidentally, it does West no good to discard a club at the third trick and then ruff a club later on. This gives up his trump trick early instead of late.

DEFENSIVE HANDS

It's harder to be a good defender than a good declarer. Since you don't see your partner's hand you don't have declarer's advantage of knowing exactly what there is to work with. And since you and your partner are not mind readers you sometimes work in different directions, whereas declarer can follow a plan without worry about interference from his partner.

As a result, average players tend to drop a trick or so in the defense of difficult hands. If you refuse to take it lying down, you can reduce this to an average of perhaps one-half trick per head—provided that your partner doesn't get in your way too much.

The average defender knows a few approved opening leads and a few general principles. The rest is guesswork.

You can do far better if you are willing to think about opening leads, to count your tricks, to use clear defensive signals with your partner, and to work out the location of the missing cards.

The Opening Lead

The first thing you learn about the opening lead is which card to lead from various combinations. For example, you are told to lead the king from a suit headed by king-queen or by ace-king. Other desirable leads are the highest card of a sequence of honors, such as the king from K-Q-J, the queen from Q-J-10, and the jack from J-10-9.

When your suit is not headed by one of these attractive combinations, you are told to lead the fourth-best card: the 5 from A-Q-6-5-2 or from K-J-9-5-3-2.

This is a good practical way to get started. When you are a beginner you must learn to lead a card with a minimum of pain and delay.

When you have acquired some experience and developed some judgment, however, you should abandon this method of choosing your opening lead.

In the great majority of hands you must listen to the bidding and choose which *suit* to lead. Only then is it proper to think about which *card* to lead.

In some cases your partner will double to tell you which suit to lead (see page 10). When your partner has bid but has not doubled, it is usually wise to lead his suit. Often he has bid the suit chiefly for this purpose.

Which card of partner's suit do you lead? With a doubleton, lead the higher card. With three or more, lead the top card from a sequence of honors; otherwise lead low from three and fourth-best from more than three.

Slam Leads

If your partner has neither bid nor doubled, lead an unbid suit against a suit slam. Preferably, lead from a suit headed by a queen or king. Your object is to set up a trick, if possible, in the hope that your side will have to be given a trick in one of the bid suits and will then be in position to cash the trick set up by the attacking opening lead.

Do not make an attacking lead against a grand slam or a small slam in notrump. Just try to avoid losing a trick by the lead; and let declarer do all of his work for himself.

Notrump Leads

If your partner has neither bid nor doubled, consider the bidding and your own hand to answer these questions:

Should you defend actively or passively?

Should you try to set up tricks for yourself or for your partner?

If the bidding indicates that the opponents have a long suit or two, you cannot afford to defend passively. Give the declarer time, and he will develop the tricks he needs.

If the opponents are unlikely to have long suits, or if your hand indicates that their long suits will break very badly, you can afford to sit back and wait for your tricks to come to you. In such hands, you try to lead from safe combinations, such as sequences of honors.

The best active defense against a notrump contract is a lead from a long suit. Lead a long suit of your own if you have a few high cards and can reasonably hope to regain the lead if you manage to establish your long suit.

If you decide to lead your long suit, lead an honor from a suit headed by a sequence of honors. Otherwise, lead the fourth-best card. You don't mind leading away from broken honors such as A-Q or K-J; if necessary, you are willing to sacrifice one trick in the suit for the sake of fast establishment.

If you decide to use the opening lead to set up your partner's suit even though he has not bid, your first choice should usually be an unbid major suit. The theory is that the opponents will usually suggest major suits to each other when they can; and their failure to do so indicates shortness—perhaps even acute shortness.

Leading Against a Suit

You cannot afford to make a lead that costs a trick when there is a trump suit. The trick won't come back, because you don't expect to run a long suit against declarer. In general, you can expect to get only the first or second trick in a side suit; after that, either declarer or the dummy will be ready to ruff.

For this reason you avoid leading away from an ace against a suit contract. You may lead the ace, but you don't lead low from the ace. (Perhaps that's why the lead in Hand No. 67 worked so well.)

If partner has bid, you lead his suit with some confidence that the lead will not cost a trick. Your confidence is sometimes misplaced, since your partner may occasionally bid a suit headed by a low card; and your lead of the ace or king may then give the opponents an unearned trick. This is one reason why good players avoid bidding a very shabby suit when the hand probably belongs to the opponents.

If partner has not bid, you tend to lead an unbid suit—particularly if you can find such a suit headed by a sequence of honors. If you have no sequence, you are willing to lead low from a king or queen. The lead from a jack is less desirable; and leading from anything lower than a jack amounts to making a neutral or passive lead.

When you have no desirable lead in an unbid suit, lead through a suit bid by dummy. This is a good idea if dummy is likely to have a broken suit of no particular length. There is little advantage in leading dummy's suit when the bidding indicates great length and strength in that suit.

A singleton makes a desirable opening lead when you have some reasonable expectation of ruffing a later round of the suit. A singleton trump is one of the worst leads ever devised by a thoughtless partner. A singleton in a side suit is almost as bad when you have no trumps or only trumps that will win tricks in their own right. The singleton is most effective when you have something like A-x or K-x-x of trumps to prevent declarer from drawing your trumps too quickly.

A doubleton is less effective as a short-suit lead. By the time you're ready to ruff, your trumps have usually been drawn. The doubleton is, however, sometimes effective as a waiting lead.

Experts lead trumps far more often than average players do. A trump makes an admirable passive lead and is a shrewd choice at a part score contract when you have broken honor holdings in the side suits.

The best time to lead a trump is when you expect dummy to do some ruffing or when you expect declarer to cross-ruff. Dummy's bidding is often very revealing of trump length and shortness in a side suit.

The Come-on Signal

When your partner is the leader you may want to tell him to continue the suit he has opened. When it is unnecessary for you to make an effort to win the trick, you may show encouragement by playing a higher card than necessary.

For example, when your partner leads the king of a suit, you might play the eight from Q-8-2 to urge him to continue the suit. Presumably, your partner has led from a suit headed by ace-king; with luck, you may take three tricks in the suit. You might play the eight, instead, from the doubleton 8-2. In this case you would hope to ruff the third round.

You would not play the eight just to show the queen or the doubleton. Your high card urges partner to lead the suit again. You would not play the eight from Q-8-2 if dummy had only two cards of the suit; nor would you play the eight from 8-2 if you preferred not to ruff.

The high card is often enough to encourage your partner to continue the suit. Sometimes you have the chance to confirm the signal by playing a lower card on a later trick. The high-low sequence of cards makes it clear to partner that you have been signalling. If you have been dealt 10-9-8 of a suit, you have to play the eight on the first round even though you have no wish to encourage a continuation. When you next play the nine, however, your partner will understand the situation.

In many such cases your partner will see a wealth of low cards in his own hand and the dummy. It should occur to him that your high card has been played by compulsion, not by choice.

The encouraging signal is most useful when you are following suit, but may also be used as a discard. For example, when declarer draws trumps, you may discard a high card in a side suit to show where your strength is. Be sure to do so only when your partner needs to know this information. Otherwise you may be giving more help to declarer than to your partner.

You can discourage your partner from continuing a suit by playing your lowest card instead of some higher card.

Other Echoes

The high-low is used defensively for two other reasons. In the trump suit a high-low, or echo, shows three trumps—usually with a desire to ruff. In a side suit, an echo is used to show an even number of cards.

The trump echo is illustrated in No. 43; the distributional echo, in No. 45.

Another important partnership weapon is the suit preference signal. This tells partner how to get the lead back to you, particularly when you are leading a card for him to ruff. In such situations, there are always two side suits other than the suit being ruffed; and one of these suits is higher-ranking than the other. You show strength in the higher suit by leading a high card for your partner to ruff; and in the lower suit, by leading the lowest possible card for partner to ruff. The principle is illustrated in No. 86.

Counting Tricks

A good defender always counts his tricks and looks for a way to increase this to the number needed to defeat the contract.

For example, when the opponent's contract is four spades, you need four tricks to defeat the contract. You bend every effort to get those four tricks. You are not interested in five tricks unless you can get the fifth trick without risking any of the first four tricks; and you are willing to give declarer an extra trick if that will improve your chance to defeat the contract.

41. HOLD THE LEAD

You all know the kind of bridge player who does everything "by the book." He can even tell you the page number for his bid or play. He's a great help to the publishing industry, but that doesn't make him a successful bridge player.

East dealer
Both sides vulnerable

NORTH
♠ 6
♡ A Q 10 9 4
♢ K 9 7
♣ Q 10 7 3

WEST
♠ K 8 7 3 2
♡ 6 5 2
♢ 10 4 2
♣ 9 4

EAST
♠ A J 9 5 4
♡ J 8 7
♢ A Q J 6
♣ 8

SOUTH
♠ Q 10
♡ K 3
♢ 8 5 3
♣ A K J 6 5 2

East	South	West	North
1 ♠	2 ♣	2 ♠	3 ♡
Pass	4 ♣	Pass	5 ♣
All Pass			

Opening lead — ♠ 3

What do the books say about the opening lead from West's hand? "Lead your partner's suit," they all say. "Unless you hold touching honors," they continue, "the correct card to lead from four or more cards is the fourth-highest card."

West had read all the books, so he led his fourth-highest spade. This allowed South to make his contract.

East could win the first trick with the ace of spades. If East failed to take the ace of diamonds promptly he wouldn't get it at all, for South would discard his losing diamonds on dummy's hearts.

Break the Rules

Fortunately for the game of bridge, the books can't tell you everything. Mind you, the books are very helpful (especially mine!) but you still have to use your own brains from time to time. You must know when to break the rules.

Take a good look at that West hand. If you lead a low spade it is clear that you can then mark time until the next hand is dealt. Your usefulness has ended with that one play.

Try leading the king of spades, however. This gives the first trick to you instead of to your partner. Now you are in position to switch to anything that looks inviting. Naturally you would shift to the ten of diamonds, and South would be down two!

Here is a little extra rule to paste in the back of your favorite bridge book: When your hand is worthless except for a high card in partner's suit, *lead that high card* instead of the usual low card. This may permit you to hold the first trick and to make a second lead after you have seen the dummy.

42. THINK BEFORE YOU LEAD

Very few players give much thought to the opening lead. Any reasonable card will do to start the play, and they begin to think only after the dummy has appeared on the table.

South dealer
Both sides vulnerable

NORTH
♠ A J 7
♡ 10 8 7 5 2
♦ A 6 5 2
♣ 5

WEST
♠ 6 5 4
♡ 4 3
♦ K Q 10 9
♣ K J 9 6

EAST
♠ 3 2
♡ A K J 9
♦ 8 7 4 3
♣ 8 4 2

SOUTH
♠ K Q 10 9 8
♡ Q 6
♦ J
♣ A Q 10 7 3

South	West	North	East
1 ♣	Pass	1 ♡	Pass
1 ♠	Pass	2 ♠	Pass
4 ♠	All Pass		

Opening lead — ♦ K

Take the West hand today, for example. If West postpones his thinking, he will lead the king of diamonds.

Declarer takes dummy's ace of diamonds, cashes the ace of clubs and ruffs a club in dummy. He ruffs a diamond in his hand and ruffs another club in dummy. And then he ruffs another diamond to reach his hand so that he can ruff a third club with dummy's last trump.

South makes five trumps in his own hand, three ruffs in the dummy, and two side aces. The total comes to ten tricks, and South is home.

Early Thought

The result is different if West thinks before he chooses his opening lead. The bidding gives the impression that South has 9 or 10 cards in the black suits.

West looks at his own hand and sees considerable length and strength in clubs. He should expect dummy to be very short in clubs.

These simple reflections should warn West that declarer will probably cross-ruff to make his contract. Since the best defense against a cross-ruff is to lead trumps at each opportunity, West should open a trump.

With a trump opening lead South is in trouble. If he ruffs only twice in dummy he will fall one trick short. South's best chance is to win the opening lead in dummy and lead a club to finesse the queen. The finesse loses, and West leads another trump, whereupon South is in even worse trouble than before.

Always consider a trump opening lead when the bidding suggests ruffing power in the dummy. You may not have time to shift to trumps later.

43. THE TRUMP ECHO

The defensive signal known as the "trump echo" is a partnership weapon. There is no value in signaling if your partner isn't watching.

East dealer
Both sides vulnerable

NORTH
♠ 9 8 3
♡ 5 2
♢ A Q 9 6
♣ Q 10 8 4

WEST
♠ 10 7 4
♡ 4
♢ J 8 7 4 2
♣ 9 7 5 2

EAST
♠ A 2
♡ A Q J 10 7 3
♢ K 5 3
♣ 6 3

SOUTH
♠ K Q J 6 5
♡ K 9 8 6
♢ 10
♣ A K J

East	South	West	North
1 ♡	Double	Pass	2 ♢
Pass	2 ♠	Pass	3 ♠
Pass	4 ♠	All Pass	

Opening lead — ♡ 4

West opened the singleton four of hearts, and East won with the ace. East returned the queen of hearts, South played the king, and West ruffed with the seven of spades.

This was the beginning of a signal, but East wasn't paying attention. East was thinking how clever he was to lead a second heart for his partner to ruff, and in the excitement he forgot to notice his partner's card.

West returned a diamond, and dummy won with the ace. Declarer promptly led a trump from dummy, and East put up the ace at once. West dropped the four of spades, completing his signal.

What the Signal Means

What do you mean when you play first high and then low in the trump suit? This "echo" in trumps means that you have a third trump.

In this case West's meaning was clear. The play of the seven and then the four of trumps meant that West still had a trump higher than the seven. East could safely lead another heart, relying on his partner to ruff higher than the dummy.

Even if East looked carefully at his trump trick, he could see that an echo had taken place. The three of spades was in dummy and the deuce of spades was in East's hand. Hence West's four of spades was West's lowest trump; and it was clear that he must have used a higher trump when he ruffed the second trick.

In short, East should have known that he could defeat the contract by leading another heart. Instead, however, East tried to get a trick with the king of diamonds. South ruffed and drew trumps, after which he easily made his game contract.

Nearly all bridge players know about the hold-up play: when an opponent leads his strong suit, you refuse the first trick—holding up your ace until a later trick. Strangely enough, those who recognize this play instantly as declarer never think of it when defending.

```
South dealer
North-South vulnerable
              NORTH
              ♠ K 5 3
              ♡ 9 4
              ◇ Q 9 8 5 4 2
              ♣ 8 4
WEST                      EAST
♠ Q 10 4                  ♠ J 8 7 6
♡ 7 5 3                   ♡ J 10 8 6
◇ 10 3                    ◇ A J 7
♣ Q J 10 9 5             ♣ 7 2
              SOUTH
              ♠ A 9 2
              ♡ A K Q 2
              ◇ K 6
              ♣ A K 6 3
```

South	West	North	East
2 NT	Pass	3 ◇	Pass
3 ♡	Pass	3 NT	All Pass

Opening lead — ♣ Q

South won the first trick with the king of clubs and promptly fired back the king of diamonds. East took the ace of diamonds —and there went the defense. South won the next club, led a diamond to the queen, and gave up a diamond. He could easily get back to dummy with the king of spades to cash the rest of the diamonds, so he had no trouble making his contract.

Error by East

South made his contract because of an error by East. When South leads the king of diamonds, East should refuse the trick. This hold-up cannot cost anything. East will surely get his ace of diamonds sooner or later.

See how the hold-up works: When South is allowed to win the first diamond trick, he continues the suit. East wins with the jack of diamonds and returns a club.

South is in no immediate danger, but he has only eight tricks. The diamond suit is shut out. Declarer can reach dummy with the king of spades to set up the diamonds, but he cannot get back to dummy to cash the rest of the suit.

In short, the hold-up play limits South to one diamond trick instead of allowing him to win four tricks in the suit. It pays to know a play that will save three tricks!

Don't be in a hurry to win the first trick of the opponent's long suit. This principle applies whether you are declarer or a defender.

45. THE DISTRIBUTIONAL ECHO

How long do you hold up? For the defenders, this question is answered by a signalling play.

South dealer
North-South vulnerable

NORTH
♠ J 6
♡ K Q J 10
♢ 7 6 3
♣ 6 5 3 2

WEST
♠ 9 5 3 2
♡ 9 6 4 2
♢ K Q 9 8
♣ 10

EAST
♠ K 8 7 4
♡ A 8 7
♢ 2
♣ J 9 8 7 4

SOUTH
♠ A Q 10
♡ 5 3
♢ A J 10 5 4
♣ A K Q

South	West	North	East
1 ♢	Pass	1 ♡	Pass
2 NT	Pass	3 NT	All Pass

Opening lead — ♠ 2

West opens the deuce of spades, covered by the jack, king and ace.

South expects to develop his diamonds. He properly leads a heart first. If the opponents are foolish enough to take the first heart trick, South will take dummy's other three hearts.

West plays the nine of hearts on the second trick, and East carefully refrains from winning with the ace.

West should play high-low when he has either two or four cards in dummy's long suit. West should play his lowest

heart, however, if he has an odd number of cards in the suit.

This signal tells East when to take his ace. In this case, East knows that West has an even number of hearts—either two or four. This means that South must have whatever is left—either four or two hearts. If South has four hearts, he cannot be shut out of dummy's suit. If South has two hearts, East must refuse the first trick but must win the second.

Signal Works

In this kind of hand, the signal works well. When East refuses the first heart trick, declarer switches to diamonds in order to take a finesse. The jack of diamonds loses to the queen, and back comes a spade.

South wins the spade and leads out the ace of diamonds. The suit breaks very badly, and South cannot afford to continue it. He leads another heart, hoping that the opponents will hold up just one trick more.

If East refused the second heart trick, declarer would have nine tricks. But East knows enough to take the ace precisely at this time. And now South goes down.

Remember this high-low signal when you are playing with a reliable partner. Be sure to give him the right signal when you have only small cards; and look for his signal when you have the ace and want to know how many tricks to hold up.

When a puppy makes a mistake, you rub his nose in it. Tournament bridge gives you a similar opportunity to break your partner (or yourself) of bad habits.

South dealer
North-South vulnerable

NORTH
♠ Q J 8 6 2
♡ Q 5
◇ A 10 9
♣ K 10 5

WEST
♠ A 7 3
♡ 6 2
◇ J 7 4 3
♣ Q 9 4 2

EAST
♠ K 10 5
♡ 8 7 4
◇ K Q 5
♣ J 8 7 3

SOUTH
♠ 9 4
♡ A K J 10 9 3
◇ 8 6 2
♣ A 6

South	West	North	East
1 ♡	Pass	1 ♠	Pass
2 ♡	Pass	2 NT	Pass
4 ♡	All Pass		

Opening lead — ♣ 2

When this hand was dealt in a recent duplicate game, the deuce of clubs was almost invariably led. The low club was played from dummy, and five or six East players committed the atrocity of putting up the jack of clubs.

This allowed South to make a hopeless contract. He won with the ace of clubs, drew trumps, and finessed dummy's ten of clubs. The finesse worked, and this was South's tenth trick.

If this happened in a game of rubber bridge nobody would think about it. West might be scolded for failing to open a diamond instead of a club. Nobody would see that East was guilty of a bridge crime.

Ask How

In a duplicate game, however, the score is there for everybody to see. Eight or nine players were defeated at a contract of four hearts. The rest made it. The unsuccessful defenders naturally ask some of the other players how it happened.

That's when East has his nose applied to his crime. At the first trick he must finesse the seven of clubs instead of putting up the jack. This is a very common position, and every player should be familiar with it.

It's a cinch that West isn't leading away from the ace of clubs on the opening lead, so South clearly has the ace. If East puts up the jack, South will surely be able to win three club tricks by finessing dummy's ten.

If East puts up the seven of clubs, South may still win three club tricks since he may have A-9 instead of A-6. But East's only chance to save a trick is to play the seven in the hope that his partner has the nine as well as the queen.

"Cover an honor with an honor," says the old rule. It was a good rule in the days of whist, but it doesn't work so well at bridge.

West dealer
North-South vulnerable

NORTH
♠ 10 9 7
♡ A J 10
◇ 10 9 7
♣ A Q 7 3

WEST
♠ K 6 4
♡ 9 7 6 2
◇ A K 5
♣ 8 6 5

EAST
♠ 5 3
♡ 8 5 4
◇ J 8 6
♣ K J 10 4 2

SOUTH
♠ A Q J 8 2
♡ K Q 3
◇ Q 4 3 2
♣ 9

West	North	East	South
Pass	Pass	Pass	1 ♠
Pass	2 NT	Pass	3 ◇
Pass	3 ♠	Pass	4 ♠
Pass	Pass	Pass	

Opening lead — ♡ 2

West opened the deuce of hearts, and dummy won with the ten. Declarer finessed the ten of spades around to West's king, took the heart return, and drew trumps, ending in the dummy.

Declarer now led the ten of diamonds from dummy.

"Cover an honor," murmured East. And he covered the ten of diamonds with his jack. This foolish play allowed South to make the contract.

South covered with the queen of diamonds, and West won with the king. Later on, South led another diamond from his hand toward dummy's nine. West couldn't prevent the nine from winning a trick, and the defenders therefore got only two diamond tricks.

Delay Is Better

What is the correct rule in such situations? Don't cover the first of "equal" cards. Wait until the last equal is led, and then cover that one if it will do your side any good.

In this case, dummy's ten and nine of diamonds were equals. When the ten is led, East should play low. This drives out West's king.

Later, dummy leads the nine of diamonds. Since this is the last of the equals, East covers with the jack. No matter how South plays, the defenders must now win three diamond tricks.

It's natural to want the best possible value for your high cards, but you mustn't let your eye for a good bargain run away with you.

North dealer
North-South vulnerable

NORTH
♠ K 6 4
♡ 8 3
♢ K J 6
♣ A Q J 7 2

WEST	EAST
♠ 8 3 2	♠ Q J 7 5
♡ A 9 6 5 2	♡ K 10 4
♢ 8 3	♢ 9 7 5 4
♣ 8 4 3	♣ K 6

SOUTH
♠ A 10 9
♡ Q J 7
♢ A Q 10 2
♣ 10 9 5

North	East	South	West
1 ♣	Pass	2 NT	Pass
3 NT	All Pass		

Opening lead — ♡ 5

West led the five of hearts, and East won with the king. East returned the ten of hearts, and South shrewdly put up the queen.

This may come as a great surprise to one and all, but the fact remains that a queen can cause a great deal of confusion. West didn't see how he could get better value than a queen, so he took the second trick with the ace of hearts.

This was the end of any effective defense.

South won the next trick with the jack of hearts and lost a club finesse to East's king. Since East was out of hearts, he had to give the lead back to declarer. South easily won the rest of the tricks, making the contract with an overtrick.

Should Have Known

West should have known what was going on when South played the queen of hearts. If East held the jack of hearts he would have led it instead of the ten. For this reason it should have been clear that South had the jack of hearts and was sure to win a heart trick.

West's best chance is to refuse the second trick, allowing South to win with the queen. Sooner or later East will win a club trick and return his last heart. Then West takes the ace of hearts and runs the rest of the suit, defeating the contract.

Strangely enough, the average player in the West seat will hold up the ace of hearts if South plays the jack at the second trick, but will be tempted to play the ace immediately if South plays the queen. A crafty declarer should play the queen in all such situations to bamboozle his opponents.

It's natural to hang on to your high cards until they're pried loose from you, but there are situations in which it pays to act the spendthrift.

North dealer
East-West vulnerable

NORTH
♠ A J 5
♡ K 9 4
◊ Q 6
♣ A Q J 8 4

WEST
♠ 8 4 2
♡ 10 6 3
◊ A 9 7 5 3
♣ 6 3

EAST
♠ 10 9 7 3
♡ J 8 7 2
◊ J 10 4
♣ K 7

SOUTH
♠ K Q 6
♡ A Q 5
◊ K 8 2
♣ 10 9 5 2

North	East	South	West
1 ♣	Pass	2 NT	Pass
3 NT	All Pass		

Opening lead — ◊ 5

West opened the five of diamonds, and South put up dummy's queen. East saw no reason to waste a high card, so he followed suit with the four of diamonds. This was a fatal error.

Declarer cashed dummy's ace of clubs to guard against a singleton king in the East hand and then led a low club. He was willing to give up a club trick to *West* but hoped to prevent East from winning a trick.

As it happened, South's precaution did him no good. East got in with his king of clubs. South had made the right play, but it didn't happen to work.

East now returned the jack of diamonds. South covered with the king of diamonds, and West won with the ace. East had to win the next diamond trick with the ten, and there was no way to get to the West hand for the rest of the diamonds.

The defenders got two diamonds and a club, but South took the rest, making his contract with an overtrick.

East Should Unblock

East should unblock the diamonds by playing the jack (or the 10) at the first trick. If East gets rid of the jack, he can lead the 10 of diamonds upon being given his club trick. South is then helpless; if he covers with the king, West can win with the ace of diamonds and then lead the nine.

How could East know that the unblocking play was necessary? East could see 17 points in the dummy and five points in his own hand. South had at least 13 points for his jump to two notrump. Since there are only 40 points in the entire deck. West could have only five points at most. This meant that West could not have a high diamond and also a high card in some side suit. There was no hope unless the diamonds could take care of themselves.

50. BLOCK OPPONENT'S SUIT

"It is a far, far better thing that I do," said the king of diamonds, "than I have ever done." Of course you don't have to believe this literally. That king of diamonds just loves to exaggerate.

South dealer
Both sides vulnerable

```
              NORTH
              ♠ Q 6 3
              ♡ 7 4 3
              ◇ A J 10 9 3
              ♣ 7 3
WEST                      EAST
♠ J 10 9 4               ♠ K 8 7
♡ Q 10 6 2               ♡ J 9 5
◇ K 8 4                  ◇ Q 6 2
♣ 8 2                    ♣ K 10 9 5
              SOUTH
              ♠ A 5 2
              ♡ A K 8
              ◇ 7 5
              ♣ A Q J 6 4
```

South	West	North	East
1 ♣	Pass	1 ◇	Pass
2 NT	Pass	3 NT	All Pass

Opening lead — ♠ J

West opened the jack of spades, and South played low from the dummy. There would be time later to try playing the queen.

South won with the ace of spades and led the five of diamonds. He intended to finesse dummy's jack. If East won with the queen, South could later run the entire diamond suit by taking another finesse.

East could stop the diamonds by refusing to win the first trick. That would allow declarer to win a trick with dummy's jack of diamonds. South would take a club finesse and get to dummy with the ace of diamonds to take another club finesse. He would thus develop four clubs, two diamonds, two hearts, and a spade.

In short, South was well on his way to making the contract, either with the diamonds in dummy or with the clubs in his own hand.

Death of a King

Naturally, the king of diamonds wasn't going to sit by idly and see this happen. Before West could tell what was going on, the king of diamonds had jumped out onto the table at the second trick.

Now South couldn't make his contract. If he won in dummy with the ace of diamonds, the suit would never come in, and he would be able to take only one club finesse. Neither long suit would produce enough tricks.

It wouldn't do South any good to refuse the first diamond. The situation would still be the same later on. In fact, if South ducked the first diamond and later tried a diamond finesse (playing West for K-Q-x of diamonds), he wouldn't make any diamond trick at all!

Whenever dummy has A-J-10-x-x of a suit behind your K-x-x or Q-x-x, remember the noble tale of the king of diamonds. Play your high card and kill dummy's suit.

51. WASTE ACE TO LEAD

"Don't waste your high cards," the beginner is told. "There's no advantage in winning a trick twice over. If your partner's card is good enough to win a trick, play low and save your own high cards for a rainy day." Good advice, provided that you can spot the exception to the rule when it comes along.

South dealer
Both sides vulnerable

NORTH
♠ K J 5 2
♡ 6
◇ K Q J 10 5
♣ 8 3 2

WEST
♠ 4
♡ K Q J 9 4
◇ A 8 4 3
♣ Q J 9

EAST
♠ Q 10 6
♡ A 8 7 5 2
◇ 9 6
♣ 7 6 5

SOUTH
♠ A 9 8 7 3
♡ 10 3
◇ 7 2
♣ A K 10 4

South	West	North	East
1 ♠	2 ♡	3 ♠	Pass
4 ♠	All Pass		

Opening lead — ♡ K

West leads the king of hearts. If East is wondering when the hostess is going to bring out the coffee, he will "automatically" play a low heart at the first trick. This automatic play will end the rubber and bring on the coffee, but East will have no reason to rejoice.

The defenders are sure to get one trump, one heart, and one diamond. They can defeat the contract only if they can also get a club trick.

See how it works out if West is allowed to win the first trick. West shifts at once to the queen of clubs, and South wins with the king. Declarer draws two rounds of trumps and leads diamonds to knock out the ace. West cannot afford to lead another club since that would give South a free finesse.

The result is that South has time to discard his low clubs on dummy's good diamonds. South makes his contract and wins the rubber.

Must Waste Ace

East must waste the ace of hearts at the first trick to defeat the contract. East then returns a club. South wins with the king, and West is able to keep his queen and jack of clubs.

South draws two rounds of trumps and forces out the ace of diamonds. West can afford to return the queen of clubs to drive out declarer's ace. Now when declarer leads a third round of diamonds from the dummy East ruffs with the queen of trumps and leads a club. The defenders thus get their club trick, defeating the contract.

52. DON'T LET A SINGLETON SCARE YOU

Defense is not an exact science. A clever declarer can put you to the guess and make you show the red badge or the white feather. Mind you, it doesn't always pay to be brave, but courage has its uses.

South dealer
East-West vulnerable

NORTH
♠ K 9 8 5 2
♡ Q J 4
◇ 3
♣ K J 5 4

WEST
♠ 7 3
♡ 9 5
◇ K 10 7 4 2
♣ 10 7 6 2

EAST
♠ 6
♡ K 10 8 7 2
◇ A 9 8 5
♣ A Q 9

SOUTH
♠ A Q J 10 4
♡ A 6 3
◇ Q J 6
♣ 8 3

South	West	North	East
1 ♠	Pass	3 ♠	Pass
4 ♠	All Pass		

Opening lead — ♡ 9

West opened the nine of hearts, dummy covered with the queen, and East's king forced out the ace. Declarer led a trump to dummy and returned the singleton diamond through East.

East timorously grabbed his ace of diamonds for fear of losing it. This play allowed South to make the contract.

East returned the ten of hearts to dummy's jack, and South got to his hand with a trump. South then led the jack of diamonds from his hand. West played low (it would have done him no good to cover with the king), and declarer discarded the losing heart from dummy.

South eventually lost two club tricks to East, but his contract was safe.

Should Play Low

East should play low when the singleton diamond is led through him. It takes courage to risk losing the ace, but this is the correct play more often than not.

In this case, South would play the jack of diamonds, and West would win with the king. This would deprive declarer of the chance to set up a diamond trick, and he would have to lose a diamond, a heart, and two clubs.

If South had the king of diamonds, East might lose the ace. In exchange, however, he would get a heart trick. East couldn't get a heart trick if he took the ace of diamonds, for then South would be able to discard the losing heart from dummy on the king of diamonds (assuming that South held the king).

In other words, it costs East nothing to play a low diamond when his partner has the king. East breaks even when South has the king.

53. LET YOUR TRUMP RIPEN

A certain kind of trump holding improves with age. Don't make the mistake of gathering it in too early.

North dealer
North-South vulnerable

NORTH
♠ A Q
♡ 8 7 4
♢ Q 9 4
♣ A K Q 7 5

WEST
♠ 8 7 5 4 2
♡ K 10 2
♢ 10 5
♣ 9 6 2

EAST
♠ 9 6 3
♡ 6
♢ A K J 8 3 2
♣ 10 4 3

SOUTH
♠ K J 10
♡ A Q J 9 5 3
♢ 7 6
♣ J 8

North	East	South	West
1 ♣	1 ♢	1 ♡	Pass
2 ♣	Pass	3 ♡	Pass
4 ♡	All Pass		

Opening lead — ♢ 10

West opened the ten of diamonds, and East overtook with the jack to win the trick. (Declarer didn't cover with dummy's queen since he hoped that West had led a singleton and that East would fail to overtake.)

East continued with the king of diamonds and then led the ace. This put South's trumps in the middle.

South ruffed with the queen of hearts, and West smugly over-ruffed with the king. West then looked around for something bright to do, but he had already muffed his one chance.

Won't Run Away

There is no need to over-ruff in this position. The king of trumps won't run away. West can afford to let declarer win the third trick with the queen of hearts.

This causes South to waste a high trump, while West maintains his position. Now West is sure to win a trump trick with the ten as well as with the king. South can take the ace of trumps, but then West has the king-ten behind the jack.

West lost his chance when he over-ruffed. South was able to draw West's two remaining trumps with the ace and the jack. Then declarer had no further problem.

Always think of this principle when you are given the chance to over-ruff with a sure trump trick. Unless you're in a hurry to make a particular play, sit tight. Your trump trick will be just as good later—and it may even be better.

54. THE UPPERCUT

Even if your partner is the best player in the world, it pays to make things easy for him. It pays even more if your partner is actually somewhat less than perfect.

North dealer
Both sides vulnerable

NORTH
♠ 7 6 3
♡ J 9 4
♢ K 3
♣ A K Q 8 3

WEST
♠ J 4
♡ A K Q 10 3 2
♢ A 10 2
♣ 9 5

EAST
♠ Q 8
♡ 7 5
♢ 9 8 6 5 4
♣ 10 6 4 2

SOUTH
♠ A K 10 9 5 2
♡ 8 6
♢ Q J 7
♣ J 7

North	East	South	West
1 ♣	Pass	1 ♠	2 ♡
Pass	Pass	3 ♠	Pass
4 ♠	Pass	Pass	Pass

Opening lead — ♡ K

West opened the king of hearts, and East began a signal by playing the seven. West saw at a glance what this meant. East and South each had doubletons in hearts. East thought his doubleton might pave the way for a ruffing trick later on, but West could tell that South would be in a position to over-ruff East.

West dismissed the ruffing trick from his mind, but came back to it after a few seconds. It was true that South would be able to over-ruff, but some good might come out of this just the same.

West continued with the queen of hearts at the second trick, and all players followed suit.

West next led the ace of diamonds. This made it obvious that the defense needed exactly one trick more, and that this trick would have to come from spades or hearts.

Key Play

West now made the key play of leading a low heart. Dummy followed with the jack, and it was clear that West wanted his partner to ruff.

East easily worked out his partner's plan. West obviously held the ace of hearts, yet he had not led it. Clearly, it was up to East to ruff. A high ruff would do more good than a low ruff, so East made the "uppercut" play of ruffing with the queen of spades.

South had to over-ruff, and then he had to give up a trick sooner or later to West's jack of spades. If East had ruffed low, South would have won with a low trump and would have drawn trumps by laying down the ace and king.

55. PROMOTE PARTNER'S TRUMPS

There's nothing very complicated about the right defense in this hand, but the average player doesn't see it. The right play is sitting there, waiting to be made, but you can show your friends all of the cards and they still won't notice it.

North dealer
North-South vulnerable

```
                NORTH
                ♠ A Q 7
                ♡ 6 5 3
                ◇ A K 6
                ♣ K 9 7 3
WEST                        EAST
♠ 10 6 5 4                  ♠ J 9 8 3 2
♡ Q 8 2                     ♡ K 9
◇ 7 3                       ◇ 8 4 2
♣ 10 8 4 2                  ♣ A Q 6
                SOUTH
                ♠ K
                ♡ A J 10 7 4
                ◇ Q J 10 9 5
                ♣ J 5
```

North	East	South	West
1 NT	Pass	3 ♡	Pass
3 NT	Pass	4 ◇	Pass
4 ♡	All Pass		

Opening lead — ♣ 2

West opens the deuce of clubs. Take it from there. How does South lose more than two clubs and a trump?

Naturally South plans to draw trumps promptly. He will get to dummy to finesse the jack of hearts, and will later get back to dummy to finesse the ten of hearts. The second finesse will work, and South will lose only one trump trick.

Try it for yourself before you read on.

Continues Clubs

East takes the first two clubs and continues with a third club.

Declarer wins the third club in dummy with the king and returns a trump. East plays the nine, and South finesses the jack.

West wins the trump finesse with the queen of hearts and leads his last club. East ruffs with the king of hearts, and South must over-ruff with the ace.

Now West's eight of hearts must sooner or later win the setting trick. East's "uppercut play" promotes his partner's trumps. But East had to look ahead and pave the way for the uppercut by continuing with the hopeless club suit.

When you're defending against notrump you must usually keep plugging away at one suit. Sometimes, however, a switch is clearly called for to stop declarer from making nine tricks.

North dealer
East-West vulnerable

```
              NORTH
              ♠ K 8 4
              ♡ A 6 4
              ◇ K Q J 9 7
              ♣ A Q
WEST                      EAST
♠ 9 3                     ♠ A Q 7 6 2
♡ J 10 9 5 2              ♡ K 3
◇ A 6 2                   ◇ 8 3
♣ 9 7 3                   ♣ 8 6 5 2
              SOUTH
              ♠ J 10 5
              ♡ Q 8 7
              ◇ 10 5 4
              ♣ K J 10 4
```

North	East	South	West
1 ◇	Pass	1 NT	Pass
3 NT	All Pass		

Opening lead — ♡ J

West opened the jack of hearts, and South considered putting up dummy's ace. He could then knock out the ace of diamonds and would be safe against any defense providing that East had the king of hearts.

South couldn't quite afford this because it was possible that West had led from a heart suit headed by K-J-10. Hence declarer played a low heart from dummy at the first trick, and East won with the king.

It was now East's turn to think. It was clear that South had the queen of hearts since the opening lead of the jack denies the queen. (If the leader's suit is headed by Q-J-10 he leads the queen rather than the jack.) If South had the ace of diamonds he would be able to win two hearts, five diamonds and at least two clubs.

East therefore came to the conclusion that the contract could not be defeated unless West held the ace of diamonds. Was it reasonable to hope that West held this card? Quite reasonable, for South could easily hold the values for a response of one notrump without having the ace of diamonds.

Low Lead Needed

All of this reasoning persuaded East to shift to a low spade. There was not enough time to set up the hearts, but spades were a different story.

South won the first spade with the jack in his own hand, but the trick did him no lasting good. He had to go after the diamonds, permitting West to take the ace. West then led his remaining spade, and East took four spade tricks to defeat the contract.

Drawing trumps is usually the declarer's job. Sometimes, however, a defender must do some of this work and must time his operation very carefully.

North dealer
East-West vulnerable

```
              NORTH
              ♠ A J 5 3
              ♡ K 10
              ◇ J 4
              ♣ A Q 10 8 3
WEST                      EAST
♠ K 10 7 6 2             ♠ Q 9 4
♡ 7 4 2                  ♡ A 5
◇ 8 5 2                  ◇ A K Q 10
♣ J 4                    ♣ 7 6 5 2
              SOUTH
              ♠ 8
              ♡ Q J 9 8 6 3
              ◇ 9 7 6 3
              ♣ K 9
```

North	East	South	West
1 ♣	1 ◇	1 ♡	Pass
1 ♠	Pass	2 ♡	Pass
3 ♡	All Pass		

Opening lead — ◇ 8

West opened the eight of diamonds, and East won the first trick with the ten. East could be pretty sure that South held four small diamonds, but there was no way to get all of the diamond tricks with trumps in the dummy.

How is East to remove the two trumps from the dummy?

The slam-bang method will not work. If East leads the ace of hearts and then his low heart, South will draw the rest of the trumps and run the clubs. He will thus make 11 tricks, fulfilling his contract with two overtricks.

Underlead Necessary

East must underlead his ace of trumps. That is, he leads his low trump, keeping the ace of trumps in his hand.

What can declarer do now? If South tries to run the clubs, West ruffs the third club and leads a trump to the ace. Then East takes the rest of the diamonds.

If declarer leads a second trump of his own accord, East takes the ace of trumps and cashes his diamonds. Either way, South must lose his contract.

58. THINK WITH PARTNER'S BRAINS

Can you think with somebody else's brains? If so, you possess empathy—a valuable quality for a bridge player to have.

South dealer
North-South vulnerable

NORTH
♠ Q 6
♡ A Q J 9 5
◇ J 9 4
♣ Q 7 4

WEST	EAST
♠ 10 5	♠ J 9 4
♡ 8 6 2	♡ 7 3
◇ A 5 2	◇ K Q 10 7
♣ K 10 6 5 3	♣ A 9 8 2

SOUTH
♠ A K 8 7 3 2
♡ K 10 4
◇ 8 6 3
♣ J

South	West	North	East
1 ♠	Pass	2 ♡	Pass
3 ♡	Pass	3 ♠	Pass
4 ♠	All Pass		

Opening lead — ♣ 5

West opened the five of clubs, and East won with the ace. East shifted to the king of diamonds and next led the seven of diamonds to West's ace. South played the six and eight of diamonds, cunningly concealing the three.

The defenders needed one more trick to defeat the contract. West's problem was whether to lead a third diamond or the king of clubs. If West guessed wrong, South would surely draw trumps and get discards on dummy's hearts.

Any reader of this column can steal a fast look at the East hand and solve West's problem with no trouble at all. When the hand was actually played, however, West couldn't steal that fast look.

How should West solve his problem logically?

What Would East Do?

West must consider what East would do with the various hands that he might hold. It is possible to work out East's length in diamonds.

Suppose East started with five diamonds. He would shift to the king of diamonds at the second trick, but would he then lead a low diamond?

East knows that West has more than two diamonds. (If West had only A-x of diamonds, he would overtake the king and return a diamond at once.) If East has five diamonds and knows that West has three diamonds, it is clear to him that South can have only two diamonds. In that case, surely, East would be eager to cash the king *and then the queen* of diamonds in order to be able to switch back to clubs after getting exactly two diamond tricks.

But East didn't continue with the queen of diamonds. Therefore, he cannot have a five-card diamond suit.

Having thought thus far with East's brains, West has solved the problem. He must lead another diamond. This defeats the contract.

[79]

59. A VIOLENT SIGNAL

It isn't always easy to make your partner lead the right suit. If a normal defensive signal isn't enough, you may have to hit your partner over the head . . . by making an abnormal discard.

South dealer
Neither side vulnerable

NORTH
♠ J 7 6 2
♡ Q J 4
◇ K 9 3
♣ 10 6 3

WEST
♠ Q 4
♡ 6 5 3
◇ A Q J 10 6 4
♣ Q 5

EAST
♠ 10 3
♡ 10 9
◇ 8 7 5 2
♣ A K 9 7 2

SOUTH
♠ A K 9 8 5
♡ A K 8 7 2
◇ None
♣ J 8 4

South	West	North	East
1 ♠	2 ◇	Pass	3 ♣
3 ♡	Pass	4 ♠	All Pass

Opening lead — ♣ Q

When this hand was played, a few years ago, Harry Fishbein led the queen of clubs from the West hand. He continued with a club to the king.

East next led the ace of clubs, and Fishbein had to find the right discard.

Fishbein couldn't see the South hand, but he knew that South was a very sound player. South had already shown up with three losing clubs; he might very well be void of diamonds. If that were the case, the contract could be defeated only if East led a fourth club. South would be unable to shut out the queen of spades.

That was good reasoning, but it was just the beginning. How could Fishbein persuade his partner to lead a fourth club?

Put yourself in his place and see if you can come up with the right answer.

Low Cards Fail

Fishbein considered the normal discards first. If he threw the four of diamonds, his lowest card in that suit, he could steer East away from a diamond return. But then East would lead a heart.

To discard a low heart would serve no useful purpose. East would then lead a diamond.

So Fishbein discarded the ace of diamonds!

This extraordinary play shook East to the marrow. Clearly Fishbein didn't want a diamond return. If he wanted a heart return, there was no need for him to be so fancy about it; a low diamond or a high heart would do the job.

East was forced to the right conclusion. His club return defeated the contract.

60. WHAT DO YOU DISCARD?

Shed a tear for poor East in this hand. If you had his hand you might make the same play—and wake up too late, as he did.

South dealer
North-South vulnerable

NORTH
♠ 8
♡ K 3 2
◇ A K Q 7 3
♣ 9 8 6 2

WEST
♠ A K Q J 6 5 3
♡ 5
◇ 8 4
♣ 7 5 3

EAST
♠ 9
♡ 8 7 6 4
◇ J 10 6 2
♣ Q J 10 4

SOUTH
♠ 10 7 4 2
♡ A Q J 10 9
◇ 9 5
♣ A K

South	West	North	East
1 ♡	4 ♠	5 ♡	Pass
6 ♡	All Pass		

Opening lead — ♠ K

West opened the king of spades and continued with the jack of spades at the second trick. Declarer naturally ruffed in dummy with the king of trumps.

East stewed for a moment or two about his discard. If he had given it a third or fourth moment, he might have come up with the right answer. As it was, he discarded the four of clubs.

South drew two rounds of trumps, and then stopped to think. If he drew two more rounds of trumps what was he going to discard from the dummy?

To avoid having to guess, South first cashed the ace and king of clubs. Then he led a diamond to dummy and ruffed a club.

This established dummy's last club, thanks to East's discard at the second trick. South thereupon drew the last two trumps, discarding low diamonds from the dummy.

Declarer could then lead a diamonds to dummy to cash the last two diamonds and the established nine of clubs.

Doleful Defender

Meanwhile East was the very picture of a doleful defender. Too late he had discovered what he should have discarded on the second spade.

As East found out, the club discard was fatal. A diamond discard would be just as bad. Declarer would easily run dummy's long suit.

East should discard a trump! Then he is in position to discard behind the dummy. If dummy discards both low diamonds, East can discard a diamond; and if dummy discards a low club, East can get rid of a club.

DECEPTIVE PLAY

It is a fine idea to make the best technical play at all times, but this is not enough to make you a great player. You must be able to steal tricks that don't belong to you.

If a contract cannot be made by straightforward play, you may be able to make it by hornswoggling an opponent. There is a special flavor to such a victory—the satisfaction of getting away with murder plus the moral (or perhaps immoral) ascendancy your larceny gives you over your trusting opponent. That opponent will be nervous and worried whenever he plays against you— even if you happen to be making perfectly innocent plays. In his effort to keep you from stealing from him, the opponent may hand you an unexpected trick.

The simplest kind of deceptive play is the *falsecard*. Often this is nothing more than playing a higher card than necessary, either to follow suit or win a trick.

For example, suppose the opening lead is the king of hearts when spades are trumps. You have Q-x of hearts in your own hand, with J-x-x in the dummy. You falsecard on the first trick by dropping your queen instead of the small card.

The idea is to create the impression that your queen is a singleton. If the opponent continues with his ace of hearts, he fears giving you the chance to ruff, whereupon dummy's jack is good for a trick.

Sometimes your opponent is not deceived, but it costs nothing to try. In most cases, the opponent will surely continue the suit if you play low; and the play of the queen gives you a chance to discourage a continuation.

Winning with a higher card than necessary is a related play. For example, suppose the opening lead is a small heart against your spade contract. Third hand puts up the queen, and you win with the ace. This may cause each defender to believe that his partner has the king of hearts. All the time, the king is nestling safely in your hand.

The same sort of play may be executed by a defender. For example, suppose you have the doubleton Q-J of trumps, sitting behind declarer. When declarer leads the ace of trumps you drop the queen. This may cause declarer to play your partner for the jack. If declarer is a born skeptic, play the jack first in such situations; he will assume that you would surely play the queen if you had both the queen and jack.

Closely related is the play in which you win a defensive trick with a card that is higher than necessary. The simplest example is No. 80, where third hand wins with the ace instead of the king.

In No. 77 and No. 73 we see more difficult examples. Here a defender wins a finesse with the ace when his queen would be good enough to take the trick.

Don't Give Yourself Away

Most deceptive plays are imaginative and hard to concoct on the spur of the moment. But they must be made quickly and naturally, since even a moment's hesitation may give you away.

Do some of your planning and thinking away from the table. Familiarize yourself with the commonest deceptive plays by reading good bridge books and your favorite daily column —and by doing some thinking of your own. That will help you recognize the situation when it occurs at the table.

Your next step is to do your thinking when it won't hurt. As a defender, you may think before making the opening lead; nobody will know just what you are thinking about.

When the dummy goes down on the table, declarer usually takes a few seconds to plan his play. This gives him the chance to plan some skullduggery without giving himself away. At the same time, both defenders should look ahead to see what is probably going to happen.

Quite apart from the need to plan a deceptive play, a defender should look to see what finesses may be taken through him and whether or not he should play high.

Remember also that silence is golden. Bridge is a social game, and sprightly conversation is a social asset, but not while a hand is in progress.

Many's the time you will lead out the ace of trumps, and the player behind you will drop a high card, such as the queen. You'll wonder if this is a false-card, until the opponent makes some annoyed comment such as "Did you have to catch it?"— and you'll know that you caught a singleton. Or perhaps the other opponent will look astonished and comment on your 7-card trump suit. If you actually have only six trumps, you'll know that the talkative opponent has given his partner away.

Incidentally, don't imagine that you can get away with a misleading remark. That would be all right at poker, but not at bridge. The bridge code of ethics is very strict on this point.

You may try to deceive an opponent by the bid you make or the card you play, but not by a remark or mannerism.

The same principle applies to giving your partner accurate information instead of giving an opponent a false picture. You must inform your partner by your bid or your play, not by your manner. The skill in bridge consists in choosing the right bid or the right play— not in developing the voice or the manner of an actor.

The safest course is to cultivate a calm appearance whether you are up to mischief or merely telling the truth. Even a bridge player can use a poker face!

61. HOLD-UP MAY DECEIVE DECLARER

If you're not in a hurry to take an ace, you may deceive your opponent.

South dealer
North-South vulnerable

NORTH
♠ K Q 10
♡ 9 5 2
◇ K J 6
♣ K J 9 6

WEST
♠ J 8 7 2
♡ J 8 6 3
◇ 10 7 4 2
♣ 3

EAST
♠ A 6 5
♡ Q 10 4
◇ 8 5 3
♣ Q 10 8 7

SOUTH
♠ 9 4 3
♡ A K 7
◇ A Q 9
♣ A 5 4 2

South	West	North	East
1 NT	Pass	3 NT	All Pass

Opening lead — ♠ 2

West opened the deuce of spades, and declarer played the king from dummy. East played the five of spades without seeming to think about it.

This was the key play of the defense. It was vital for East to refuse the first trick without making a fuss about it.

Declarer tried the clubs by taking the ace and king, but the suit broke badly. Now South needed a second spade trick to make his contract. He got to his hand with a diamond and led a spade toward dummy. West played low, and South had to guess whether to play the queen or the ten from dummy.

Because of East's casual play at the first trick, South guessed wrong. Assuming that *West* had the ace of spades, South played dummy's queen.

This time, of course, East took his ace. He returned a spade, and West took two more spade tricks. South eventually went down one instead of making his vulnerable game.

There would be a different story to tell if East took the ace of spades at the first trick. South would later finesse dummy's ten of spades, and would easily make his contract.

How Did East Know?

How did East know that he should refuse the first trick? How can a player look ahead so quickly?

The answer is that East didn't look ahead and didn't know. He didn't need to. He saw that his ace was behind K-Q-10 and therefore *automatically* refused the first trick.

This is a good rule to follow, especially when defending against a notrump contract. When you have the ace behind dummy's K-Q-10, don't think *and don't hesitate*. Refuse the first trick in that suit and keep an innocent look on your face. This may cost you a trick once every ten years, but it will pay big dividends in the long run.

How do you prevent an opponent from taking a successful finesse? Make him believe that some other play is safer.

South dealer
Both sides vulnerable

NORTH
♠ K Q J 9
♡ A 6
♢ 7 4
♣ A Q 7 5 2

WEST
♠ 6 4
♡ 10 3
♢ A 10 9 6 2
♣ K 10 9 8

EAST
♠ 8 7 5 2
♡ 9 5 4 2
♢ J 5 3
♣ 4 3

SOUTH
♠ A 10 3
♡ K Q J 8 7
♢ K Q 8
♣ J 6

South	West	North	East
1 ♡	Pass	2 ♣	Pass
2 NT	Pass	3 ♠	Pass
3 NT	Pass	6 NT	All Pass

Opening lead — ♡ 10

When this hand was played in a team match, recently, the final contract was six notrump, and the play went much the same way for the first few tricks at both tables.

West opened the 10 of hearts, and declarer took the king and ace to make sure that the hearts were going to run. With nine sure tricks in spades

and hearts, declarer needed two diamonds and one club or two clubs and one diamond.

Which play should he try?

At the first table, declarer led a diamond from the dummy and put up the king from his hand. West won with the ace of diamonds and led a spade.

South could tell he was going to get only one diamond, so he had to try for two clubs. He therefore led a club from his hand and finessed dummy's queen. The finesse worked, and South spread his hand and claimed his twelve tricks.

Better Defense

There was better defense at the other table, where the West player was Sidney Lazard of New Orleans. When declarer led a low diamond from dummy and put up the king from his hand, Lazard was ready with the deuce of diamonds.

Now South didn't know what was going on. He could still switch to clubs, but he had no reason to do so. For all he knew, the ace of diamonds was held by East.

So this declarer went over to dummy with a spade and led another diamond towards his hand. East played low, and South put up the queen. Now Lazard took the ace of diamonds and led another diamond to his partner's jack to defeat the slam.

The best way to prevent an opponent from refusing a trick is to scare him.

North dealer
North-South vulnerable

NORTH
♠ 8 3
♡ K 9 6 4
♢ A Q J 7 6
♣ A 8

WEST
♠ J 9 7 4 2
♡ 5 2
♢ 8 3 2
♣ 6 4 2

EAST
♠ A Q 6
♡ J 10 8 3
♢ K 5
♣ J 10 9 5

SOUTH
♠ K 10 5
♡ A Q 7
♢ 10 9 4
♣ K Q 7 3

North	East	South	West
1 ◊	Pass	2 NT	Pass
3 NT	All Pass		

Opening lead — ♠ 4

West opens the four of spades. What happens from here on depends on how good the players are.

In the average game, East wins the first trick with the ace of spades and leads back the queen of spades. If South is a good player, he refuses that second trick. East continues with his last spade, and South wins with the king.

South has "held up" his king of spades to exhaust all spades held by East. His hold-up play will pay big dividends.

South takes the diamond finesse, losing to East's king.

East cannot lead a spade because he doesn't have a spade to lead. Whatever East may return, South will win the rest of the tricks, making the contract plus an overtrick.

East Can Be the Hero

East can be the hero of the hand at the very first trick. Instead of winning the first trick with the ace of spades, East should play the *queen!*

What can East lose by this play? If *West* has the king of spades, the queen is as good a card as the ace. If *South* has the king of spades, he will surely win a trick with it eventually.

To see what East can gain, look at the first trick from South's point of view. South doesn't know who has the ace of spades. It is quite possible that West has led from a long suit headed by ace-jack. If so, South must take his king of spades immediately or he will never get it at all. In short, East's first play should scare South into winning the first trick.

Now South must try the diamond finesse, losing to East's king. East cashes the ace of spades and leads his other spade, whereupon West defeats the contract with his long suit.

Look for this kind of play when you are in third position against a notrump contract. If you have A-Q-x or A-J-x, play your middle card at the first trick instead of taking the ace. This will scare declarer away from the hold-up.

If you're a student of finesses add the fake finesse to your little book.

East dealer
North-South vulnerable

NORTH
♠ Q 10 6 5
♡ J 5 2
◇ Q 8 4
♣ K 6 3

WEST
♠ 8 2
♡ K 10 8
◇ 7 6 3
♣ J 10 9 7 2

EAST
♠ 7
♡ A 9 7 6
◇ 10 9 5 2
♣ A Q 8 4

SOUTH
♠ A K J 9 4 3
♡ Q 4 3
◇ A K J
♣ 5

East	South	West	North
Pass	1 ♠	Pass	2 ♠
Pass	4 ♠	All Pass	

Opening lead — ♣ J

West opened the jack of clubs, and South could see almost at once that he could not make the hand by force. He knew that the ace and king of hearts were in different hands.

The opening lead made it clear that East held the ace and queen of clubs. East could not also hold both top hearts since he had never entered the bidding. If West had held both top hearts he would have opened the king of hearts.

South wasn't a bit happy to discover that the top hearts were split, since this meant that

his contract could not be made unless the opponents made a mistake.

Try a normal play in hearts to see what happens. Lead a low heart from the South hand. West plays low, and East captures the jack. Then West has K-10 of hearts behind the queen and must make two additional heart tricks.

The same thing is true if declarer leads a low heart from the dummy. East plays low, and West captures the queen with the king. Now East has the A-9 of hearts behind dummy's jack and must make two further heart tricks.

Cunning Play

There is a cunning play to use in this situation. You must persuade the opponents that you want to take a finesse that is going to lose. They will open the doors for you, only to discover that you have stolen a trick from them.

In this case, South ruffed the second round of clubs, drew trumps with the ace and queen, and then led the jack of hearts from dummy. East thought that South had hearts headed by the K-10 and that he was going to lose a finesse to a queen in the West hand. East therefore played a low heart, and the jack forced out West's king of hearts.

It was a simple matter to return to dummy with the queen of diamonds and lead another heart toward the queen to set up the vital tenth trick.

65. HOW TO GET A TRUMP LEAD

A good opponent will try to thwart your plans. Give him the wrong plan to thwart.

South dealer
North-South vulnerable

```
              NORTH
              ♠ K 3
              ♡ A J
              ◇ 8 7 4 2
              ♣ K 10 9 4 2
WEST                      EAST
♠ J 5 2                   ♠ A 7 4
♡ K Q 10 7                ♡ 9 8 6 4 2
◇ J 10 6 3                ◇ 9 5
♣ 8 5                     ♣ Q J 6
              SOUTH
              ♠ Q 10 9 8 6
              ♡ 5 3
              ◇ A K Q
              ♣ A 7 3
```

South	West	North	East
1 ♠	Pass	2 ♣	Pass
2 ♠	Pass	3 ♠	Pass
4 ♠	Pass	Pass	Pass

Opening lead — ♡ K

West opened the king of hearts, and South considered the hand as a whole before he made his first play from the dummy. This, incidentally, is a fine idea; it gives you the chance to look several tricks ahead and to make your deceptive plays without apparent thought.

In this case, South saw that he would have to lose a heart,

a club and a trump. The trouble was that he might also lose a second trump trick.

Instead of trying to guess who had the jack of spades, South decided to give the opponents the chance to take the guess for him. He won the first trick with the ace of hearts and led the jack right back.

West's Assumption

West won with the queen of hearts and assumed that South wanted to ruff hearts in the dummy. Why else would declarer lead the jack of hearts at the second trick?

What do you do, as a defender, when declarer tries to ruff in dummy? You lead trumps to reduce dummy's ruffing power. And that's just what West did.

West led a low trump, dummy played low, and East won with the ace. This was just what South wanted, of course. He could now draw trumps without further loss, and his game contract was safe.

This is a device worth remembering. If you make it seem that you are going to ruff losers in the dummy, the opponents will usually lead trumps for you.

[88]

Several old rules of play have come down to us from the days of whist. These are good general guides for the beginner, but the experienced player cannot blindly rely on them.

South dealer
Both sides vulnerable

NORTH
♠ J 9 2
♡ Q 10 4
◇ Q 10 6 3
♣ 10 9 4

WEST
♠ A 8 6 3
♡ 9 6 5 2
◇ 8 7 4
♣ K 5

EAST
♠ Q 7 5 4
♡ 8 7 3
◇ A 5
♣ 8 7 3 2

SOUTH
♠ K 10
♡ A K J
◇ K J 9 2
♣ A Q J 6

South	West	North	East
2 NT	Pass	3 NT	Pass
Pass	Pass		

Opening lead — ♠ 3

West opened the three of spades, and South craftily played the jack from dummy. This was a very neat little trap, and East fell into it by playing the queen of spades.

East didn't realize that he was making the wrong play. One old rule told him to cover an honor with an honor. An-other old rule told him to play "third hand high." East relied on these rules when he put up the queen of spades.

South won with the king of spades, of course, and now had a second spade stopper. He led diamonds to force out the ace, since then he was sure to win two spades, three hearts, three diamonds, and at least one club. For safety's sake, he didn't try the club finesse, since his game contract was sure without this play.

Correct Play

The correct play at the first trick defeats the contract. East should not put up the queen of spades. He should content himself with some such encouraging card as the seven.

East knows that South has only two spades if West has led a legitimate fourth-best. If South held A-x, he would surely play the nine of spades rather than the jack of spades from dummy at the first trick. If South holds the doubleton king of spades, East cannot gain anything by playing the queen.

If East plays low at the first trick, the defenders will be able to take three spades, the ace of diamonds, and the king of clubs. These five tricks defeat the contract.

Whenever bridge fans talk about deceptive plays, I think back 20 years or so to a hand in which Josephine Culbertson gave Hal Sims the works—in spades.

West dealer
East-West vulnerable

NORTH
♠ K J 3
♡ 7
♢ A Q 7 4
♣ K Q 9 4 2

WEST
♠ A 5 4
♡ 8 4 3 2
♢ K 9 6
♣ A 10 7

EAST
♠ Q 10 7 6
♡ 10 5
♢ J 10 5 3 2
♣ 6 3

SOUTH
♠ 9 8 2
♡ A K Q J 9 6
♢ 8
♣ J 8 5

West	North	East	South
Pass	1 ♣	Pass	1 ♡
Pass	2 ♢	Pass	3 ♡
Pass	3 NT	Pass	4 ♡
All Pass			

Opening lead — ♠ 4

The hand was played in the 1935 match between Mr. and Mrs. Ely Culbertson and Mr. and Mrs. P. Hal Sims. The Culbertsons won handily.

North should open with one diamond and later bid the clubs, thus promising only the value of a normal opening bid. As the bidding actually went, it became clear that North had moderate spade strength in addition to clubs and diamonds,

and also that South didn't want to play notrump nohow. This gave Mrs. Culbertson the brilliant but unorthodox idea of leading a low spade.

Sims confidently played a low spade from the dummy. He felt sure that East had the ace of spades. If East had ace-queen-ten, nothing could be done. If East had ace-ten, he might make the mistake of taking the ace instead of playing the ten.

It was a good idea, but it didn't work. Ely Culbertson put up the ten of spades without hesitation, winning the trick. Culbertson returned the six of clubs to his partner's ace. And now Mrs. Culbertson led her other small spade!

Time Out for Thought

Sims took time out for thought. A burly giant of a man, he glared at his petite opponent. What was she doing to him?

Impossible, he decided. She didn't have nerve enough to give him the works. So he played the jack of spades from dummy, feeling sure that the lead was from the queen and that Culbertson had the ace.

As it happened, the cards were just the other way. Culbertson triumphantly won with the queen of spades and returned another spade to his wife's ace. It was a David-Goliath contest, but in this case Goliath survived the battle to congratulate his opponent for a brilliant stratagem.

68. DISCOURAGE A FINESSE

When it comes to headaches, it's better to give than to receive. What's more, don't be slow. For best results, deliver that headache at the earliest possible moment.

North dealer
North-South vulnerable

NORTH
♠ A Q
♡ A Q 10 7
◇ A K 6 5 2
♣ K Q

WEST
♠ K 9 6 2
♡ 3
◇ Q J 9 7 3
♣ A 10 8

EAST
♠ 10 8 7 5 3
♡ 4 2
◇ 8
♣ J 7 6 5 2

SOUTH
♠ J 4
♡ K J 9 8 6 5
◇ 10 4
♣ 9 4 3

North	East	South	West
2 ◇	Pass	2 NT	Pass
3 NT	Pass	4 ♡	Pass
6 ♡	All Pass		

Opening lead — ♠ 9

What should West lead against the excellent contract of six hearts? West knows that the diamonds will break very badly. West also knows that dummy will come down with a very strong hand, including all of the missing aces.

In short, West knows that his king of spades is probably in finessable position. The best way to wriggle out of this position is to force South to make up his mind before he knows

much about the hand.

West gives declarer a headache by leading the nine of spades.

What is South to do? The spade finesse gives him an even chance for the contract. If he refuses the spade finesse and tries to set up a diamond, the odds are more than 5 to 1 in his favor.

South's "correct" play, therefore, is to put up the ace of spades and lead out both top diamonds. If nothing bad happens, South can ruff a diamond, get to dummy with a trump, and ruff another diamond. One more trump to dummy, and declarer will be in position to cash the last diamond and discard the losing spade.

Unfortunately for South, the "correct" play runs into misery. East ruffs the second diamond and leads a spade. Now the defenders get three tricks, defeating the contract by two tricks.

Delay Would Fail

The defense would fail if West delayed the headache. For example, suppose West opens a diamond. Dummy wins, and South draws two rounds of trumps. He then leads a diamond to the ace, intending to go ahead with that suit.

When East discards on the second diamond, it becomes clear that the suit is hopeless. Hence South must fall back on a spade finesse, and now he makes his contract.

69. A DECEPTIVE OPENING LEAD

When you miss your chance to deceive an opponent at a tournament, your wasted opportunity will not be entirely forgotten. Somebody else may make the right play, and you're sure to hear all about it.

West dealer
North-South vulnerable

NORTH
♠ 8 6
♡ K 9 8 5 2
♢ 9 5
♣ K J 7 3

WEST	EAST
♠ 9 7 2	♠ A J 10 5 4
♡ A 7 6 3	♡ Q J 10 4
♢ J 6 3	♢ 10 7 4
♣ A Q 6	♣ 4

SOUTH
♠ K Q 3
♡ None
♢ A K Q 8 2
♣ 10 9 8 5 2

West	North	East	South
Pass	Pass	1 ♠	2 ♢
2 ♠	Pass	Pass	3 ♣
Pass	4 ♣	Pass	5 ♣
Pass	Pass	Pass	

Opening lead — ♣ A

The hand was played 13 times, and each time South was declarer at a contract of five clubs. The contract was fulfilled 12 times and defeated once.

At 12 tables, West made the routine opening of a spade.

East won with the ace and returned the jack of spades. South won and led the ten of clubs for a finesse. West could get his ace of clubs, but South later finessed for the queen and thus made his contract.

Thirteenth Table

The play went quite differently at the thirteenth table. West opened the ace of clubs. At the second trick, West led a low club.

South chewed this over in his mind for quite a while. Why was West so intent on leading trumps? Perhaps he had length in diamonds and wanted to reduce dummy's ruffing power.

It never occurred to declarer that West had led from A-Q-x of trumps. South finally put up dummy's king of clubs at the second trick—and this cost him the contract. He was now sure to lose a second trump trick.

South made a good try for his contract by running the diamonds in order to discard dummy's spades. But that still left dummy with only two trumps, while South had three spades.

How did West think of his strange opening lead? The lead could cost nothing, he explained. If dummy had the king, West would continue for deceptive purposes. If dummy did not have the king of clubs, West could shift to a different suit and wait for his second trump trick.

What equipment do you need for a game of bridge? A couple of decks of cards, a scorepad, a pencil, and so forth. You might also need a 12-inch ruler, preferably of some heavy wood.

North dealer
North-South vulnerable

NORTH
♠ A Q J 3
♡ A
♢ A 6 3 2
♣ 10 8 3 2

WEST
♠ 8 7 5
♡ 6 5 4 2
♢ Q J 10 9
♣ 6 5

EAST
♠ K 10 9 4
♡ 8 7 3
♢ K 5
♣ Q J 9 7

SOUTH
♠ 6 2
♡ K Q J 10 9
♢ 8 7 4
♣ A K 4

North	East	South	West
1 ♢	Pass	1 ♡	Pass
1 ♠	Pass	3 ♡	Pass
4 ♡	All Pass		

Opening lead — ♢ Q

You are East. Your partner opens the queen of diamonds, and dummy wins with the ace. Naturally you drop the king of diamonds on this trick to unblock your partner's suit.

Declarer cashes the ace of hearts, leads a club to the king, and then draws three more rounds of trumps, discarding low diamonds from the dummy. On the fourth trump you nonchalantly discard the four of spades.

South next leads a low spade and finesses dummy's queen. Naturally, since you are a very fine player, you drop the nine of spades.

The idea is to persuade South that his finesse has succeeded. Perhaps he will be foolish enough to get back to his hand with the ace of clubs and finesse the jack of spades. Then you will pounce on the trick with your king of spades, and South will be down! He will lose a spade, two diamonds, and a club.

Watch Out for Partner

In a case of this sort you must watch out for your partner. When declarer finesses dummy's queen of spades, your partner may reach out for the trick—making it clear that he expects you to win with the king.

This is, of course, a dead giveaway. Declarer will not take a second spade finesse, and your plot will fail. (An expert declarer would not take a second finesse anyway, but that's another story.)

How do you prevent your partner from reaching across the table, thus giving you away?

That's what the ruler is for. One sharp rap over the knuckles will remind your partner not to reach for a trick next time. (Incidentally, don't have more than one ruler in the house or your partner may have one on the other side of the table.)

[93]

The easiest way to deceive an opponent is to conceal something from him. No concealment is possible with the dummy, for all of dummy's cards are exposed, but you can still use the dummy to deceive an opponent.

South dealer
North-South vulnerable

NORTH
♠ 6 3
♡ J 5
◇ A J 10 9 6
♣ K 10 5 3

WEST	EAST
♠ Q 8 7 4 2	♠ K J 5
♡ A 6 2	♡ K 9 8 4
◇ 7 3 2	◇ 8 4
♣ Q 6	♣ 9 8 4 2

SOUTH
♠ A 10 9
♡ Q 10 7 3
◇ K Q 5
♣ A J 7

South	West	North	East
1 NT	Pass	3 NT	Pass
Pass	Pass		

Opening lead — ♠ 4

West opened the four of spades, and East held the first trick with the king. East continued with the jack of spades, holding that trick also. East then led his last spade, and South at last took the ace.

Dummy was out of spades by this time and had to make a discard. What should be discarded from dummy on the third spade?

Obviously not a diamond, since all of the diamonds are good tricks. The straightforward discard is a heart, for then South can keep all of dummy's clubs and perhaps can win four club tricks.

A heart discard makes it rather clear that South has no interest in the heart suit. This makes it easy for East to throw a heart or two away, and South must guess the location of the queen of clubs in order to make the game.

Discards a Club

When the hand was actually played, South didn't have to guess. On the third round of spades, South threw a small club from dummy. This made it look as though he had very little interest in the clubs.

Mind you, this wasn't a sure-fire maneuver, guaranteed to deceive the shrewdest opponent. Nevertheless, this simple play of discarding from the suit that you really want will fool the enemy more often than not.

In this case, it had a great success. East had to discard on the third round of diamonds, and who can blame him for throwing a club rather than a heart? He also had to discard on the fourth diamond, and he then threw another club.

Naturally South had no further trouble in finding the queen of clubs and in making the game and rubber.

Deceptive discards have a special flavor since most bridge players would rather steal a trick than earn one.

South dealer
North-South vulnerable

NORTH
♠ J 8 7 5
♡ A Q 6
♢ J 5
♣ K J 6 5

WEST
♠ K 6
♡ J 10 9 5
♢ K 7 6 2
♣ 8 7 4

EAST
♠ 3
♡ 8 4 3 2
♢ A 10 9 4 3
♣ 10 3 2

SOUTH
♠ A Q 10 9 4 2
♡ K 7
♢ Q 8
♣ A Q 9

South	West	North	East
1 ♠	Pass	3 ♠	Pass
6 ♠	All Pass		

Opening lead — ♡ J

West opens the jack of hearts, and you thank your lucky stars that he didn't get his fingers on a diamond. It was very careless of you to deal the ace and king of diamonds to the opponents only a minute or so before you bid a slam.

Thanks to the opening lead, your slam is cold if the spade finesse works. There are at least four ways to play the hand, and the choice depends partly on your own temperament and partly on what you think of West.

One reasonable plan is to win the heart and cash the ace of spades. Perhaps the king will drop. If it doesn't, run the hearts, discarding a diamond. Then try the clubs, hoping to discard another diamond by the time the king of trumps is played. This will work if the player with the king of spades has three or more clubs.

If You Finesse

The other three plans are used if you finesse in spades. One plan is to win the first trick with the ace of hearts and take the spade finesse. If West wins, he may fail to lead a diamond.

A second plan is to run the three hearts, discarding a diamond. Then you try the spade finesse. If the finesse loses, however, West will surely return a diamond.

Probably the best plan is to run the three hearts, discarding the nine of clubs! Then try the spade finesse. If it loses, West will surely return a club. And then you will draw trumps and get rid of your diamonds on dummy's clubs.

This is the best plan not only because it will almost surely work against most opponents. Equally important is the fact that a swindle of this sort will give you the laugh on West for at least a year. This may be worth thousands of points if you play against that particular West very often.

73. FINESSES DON'T ALWAYS WORK

According to Poor Alfred's Almanac, Christmas comes but once a year. If an opponent acts like Santa Claus at any other time maybe you ought to tug at his whiskers and find out if he's for real.

South dealer
North-South vulnerable

```
              NORTH
              ♠ K J 10 8
              ♡ 5 4
              ◇ J 3
              ♣ A J 10 9 4
WEST                      EAST
♠ 6 5 3                   ♠ A Q 4
♡ J 10 9 8 3             ♡ 7 6 2
◇ 4 2                     ◇ K Q 10 9 7
♣ Q 8 7                   ♣ 5 2
              SOUTH
              ♠ 9 7 2
              ♡ A K Q
              ◇ A 8 6 5
              ♣ K 6 3
```

South	West	North	East
1 NT	Pass	2 ♣	Pass
2 ◇	Pass	3 NT	All Pass

Opening lead — ♡ J

South won the first trick with the queen of hearts and returned a spade to finesse dummy's jack. East won with the *ace* of spades and returned the king of diamonds.

Since nobody had told South about Christmas he thought he saw snowflakes and reindeer.

He pounced on the diamond with his ace and tried another spade finesse, expecting to win three spades, three hearts, a diamond and at least two clubs.

It was all a mirage. East won with the queen of spades, the deceptive wretch, and ran four diamond tricks to collect a penalty of 200 points.

Good Question

"How could I tell what was going on?" South asked plaintively when the hand was over. It was a good question, but it came too late to do South any good.

South could tell what was going on if he gave East credit for being some sort of bridge player. If East had A-x or A-x-x of spades he wouldn't win the first spade trick. He would let dummy win the first spade, after which South would have to use up an entry to get back to his hand for another spade finesse.

This is standard defensive play, and a good player who takes the first spade trick in this situation either has a singleton ace or is executing some kind of hipper-dipper.

If East is known to be a good player, perhaps he should refuse the first spade trick and win the next spade with the ace! If South fell for this plot he would be entitled to sympathy.

Everybody knows about counting points during the bidding. The next step is to count them during the play of the cards as well.

South dealer
North-South vulnerable

NORTH
♠ A 5
♡ A J
◇ 6 3 2
♣ Q 10 7 6 5 4

WEST
♠ J 9 7 4 2
♡ 7 5 2
◇ 10 8 5
♣ 8 2

EAST
♠ K 10 6 3
♡ 10 8 6 3
◇ K 9 4
♣ K J

SOUTH
♠ Q 8
♡ K Q 9 4
◇ A Q J 7
♣ A 9 3

South	West	North	East
1 NT	Pass	3 NT	All Pass

Opening lead — ♠ 4

West led the four of spades, and South took the customary pause to plan his play. East used this time to do some counting and planning of his own.

East could see 11 points in high cards in the dummy and 10 points in his own hand. He gave declarer credit for about 17 points for the strong opening bid of one notrump. This left only about 2 of the 40 points in the deck for West to hold.

It happened that South had 18 points, which left only 1

point for West. South might have held only 16 points, and then West would have held 3 points. East assumed the middle value, knowing that he might be 1 point away from the truth.

What was the importance of this counting? East knew that his partner had a virtually worthless hand and that South could almost surely make his contract by developing the diamonds. East was therefore on the alert for a way to steer declarer away from the diamond finesse.

Clears Spades

By this time, declarer had made his plan. He played a low spade from dummy at the first trick, and East won with the king. East returned the three of spades, and the queen and ace of spades fell together. West followed suit with the deuce of spades, confirming the fact that he had opened from a five-card suit.

Declarer next led a low club from dummy, and East played the king! South won with the ace of clubs and triumphantly led the nine of clubs for a finesse through West. East pounced on this trick with the jack of clubs and gave his partner three additional spade tricks, defeating the contract.

If the king of clubs had not "dropped," South would have entered dummy twice with hearts for two diamond finesses. This would have given him ten tricks.

75. STEALING A TRICK

You might not think that you can do much with the diamonds in this hand, but they lend themselves to a very neat deceptive play.

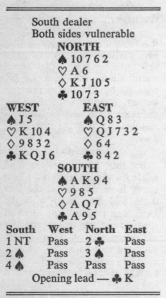

South dealer
Both sides vulnerable

NORTH
♠ 10 7 6 2
♡ A 6
♢ K J 10 5
♣ 10 7 3

WEST
♠ J 5
♡ K 10 4
♢ 9 8 3 2
♣ K Q J 6

EAST
♠ Q 8 3
♡ Q J 7 3 2
♢ 6 4
♣ 8 4 2

SOUTH
♠ A K 9 4
♡ 9 8 5
♢ A Q 7
♣ A 9 5

South	West	North	East
1 NT	Pass	2 ♣	Pass
2 ♠	Pass	3 ♠	Pass
4 ♠	Pass	Pass	Pass

Opening lead — ♣ K

West opened the king of clubs, and South refused the first trick.

West continued with the queen of clubs, and South won with the ace. Declarer next laid down the ace and king of spades, concealing his relief when the suit broke normally. A bad trump break would have been too much for South to survive.

At this stage it looked like the kind of hand you play in your sleep. You run the diamonds, hoping that the player with the last trump has at least three diamonds. If so, he has to follow suit, and you can run the fourth diamond to discard the last club. You don't care if the opponent ruffs at that time, for you still get your discard.

The trouble is that the opponent's ruff may come too soon. In today's hand, for example, East would ruff the third diamond and lead a club. The defenders would then get two clubs, a trump, and a heart, defeating the contract.

Expert Stays Awake

When Terence Reese held the South cards, he didn't play the hand in his sleep. After drawing two rounds of trumps, he led out the ace and king of diamonds and then led the jack of diamonds from dummy.

It all looked very familiar to East. He thought South had started with ace and one small diamond. If so, the jack of diamonds was a loser, and there was no need for East to ruff it.

East therefore discarded a heart on the jack of diamonds and woke up with a start when Reese produced the queen of diamonds to win the trick. Having sneaked the third round of diamonds through, Reese got back to dummy with the ace of hearts to lead the fourth diamond. It didn't matter when East ruffed at this stage, for Reese could get rid of his last club. It was then easy to make the game contract.

[98]

A certain kind of bird is said to pretend it has a broken wing. It leads hunters away from its nest and then flies away, cackling as it goes. More or less the same thing happened on this hand, including the cackle.

South dealer
Both sides vulnerable

NORTH
♠ J 10 3
♡ J 10 7
♢ K Q
♣ Q 10 9 7 3

WEST
♠ K 8 6 4 2
♡ A 6 2
♢ 9 5 2
♣ K 4

EAST
♠ 7 5
♡ K Q 8 4
♢ 10 7 6 4 3
♣ 6 2

SOUTH
♠ A Q 9
♡ 9 5 3
♢ A J 8
♣ A J 8 5

South	West	North	East
1 NT	Pass	3 NT	Pass
Pass	Pass		

Opening lead — ♠ 4

West opened the four of spades, and declarer put up the jack from dummy. East played low, and South put on the broken-wing act by playing the

queen of spades from his own hand. This made it look as though he had only the doubleton ace-queen of spades.

South next entered dummy with a diamond in order to try the club finesse. West won with the king of clubs and promptly returned a low spade to take advantage of South's short holding.

Much to West's surprise, declarer came out from behind the bushes by winning the trick with the nine of spades. Then South ran a total of ten tricks before giving up the lead again.

Switch Beats Contract

A switch to hearts would, of course, beat the contract. This is just what South feared, and it was what inspired his broken-wing act.

If South had won the first trick with dummy's jack of spades, it would have been clear to West that he could get nowhere by leading spades. On winning with the king of clubs, West would switch to hearts, and the defenders would take four hearts to defeat the game contract.

77. CONCEAL YOUR STRENGTH

There are two kinds of luck—what you suffer from and what the opponents fall into. The only redeeming feature of this is that the opponents don't always know what a bed of roses they have stumbled upon. Don't tell them!

South dealer
Both sides vulnerable

NORTH
♠ 10 9 7 6
♡ 6 3
♦ A Q
♣ 10 9 6 5 2

WEST
♠ 8 5 2
♡ A Q 2
♦ J 10 9 7
♣ 8 4 3

EAST
♠ K J 4 3
♡ 4
♦ 8 6 5 4 2
♣ A J 7

SOUTH
♠ A Q
♡ K J 10 9 8 7 5
♦ K 3
♣ K Q

South	West	North	East
1 ♡	Pass	1 NT	Pass
4 ♡	All Pass		

Opening lead — ◇ J

South bounced into four hearts without really knowing what he could make. It was a reasonable bid, but he also found a useful dummy.

West opened the jack of diamonds, and dummy won with the queen. South wondered whether to finesse in trumps or in spades, and he properly decided to try the heart finesse first. If it lost to the queen, he could get back to dummy with the ace of diamonds to try the spade finesse.

This was a reasonable plan and might well have succeeded. If West had been fuming about the luck of his opponents, he would have won the first trump trick with the queen of hearts. South would eventually get to dummy for a spade finesse, and would lose two trumps and one club.

Foresight

West didn't waste his time fuming. He could see that if South needed a spade or club finesse it would work. West made up his mind to conceal this fact from South.

Therefore West won the trump trick with the *ace* instead of the queen. The diamond return put declarer back in the dummy.

South didn't know about the spades, but he did know that the trump finesse had worked. So he led another trump from dummy, and East's discard was like a cold shower. South had to lose a second trump trick, a club and a spade.

78. PAINT A FALSE PICTURE

When you play a hand, you don't know where all of the missing high cards are. Always remember that your opponents suffer from the same handicap. You can win many an "impossible" trick if you paint a false picture for an opponent to stare at.

North dealer
North-South vulnerable

NORTH
♠ 10 7 3
♡ J 6
♢ A K Q 10 9
♣ K 4 3

WEST
♠ K 6 4
♡ 10 9 8 4
♢ 7 3 2
♣ A Q 2

EAST
♠ 5 2
♡ K 7 5 2
♢ 6 5 4
♣ J 9 8 5

SOUTH
♠ A Q J 9 8
♡ A Q 3
♢ J 8
♣ 10 7 6

North	East	South	West
1 ♢	Pass	1 ♠	Pass
2 ♢	Pass	3 ♠	Pass
4 ♠	All Pass		

Opening lead — ♡ 10

Put yourself in the West seat and defend against four spades. You open the ten of hearts, hoping to strike a favorable position in the suit.

Declarer puts up the jack of hearts from dummy, East covers with the king, and South wins with the ace. This tells you that South has the queen of hearts as well, since East

would play the queen instead of the king if he had both honors.

South next leads a diamond to dummy and returns the ten of spades for a finesse. You win with the king of spades and must think of something new. What is your next play?

Switch Is Vital

A switch is vital, since you can see what will happen if you lead another heart: Declarer will win the rest of the trumps, the rest of the diamonds and at least two hearts for at least 11 tricks.

You need three club tricks to defeat the contract—but you can't possibly get them. That is, you can't win three club tricks if declarer knows what you know.

The point is that South doesn't know who has the ace of clubs. If you switch to the queen of clubs, South will probably play a low club from dummy instead of putting up the king. He will assume that the lead is from Q-J, in which case his best bet is to duck the first trick.

Your next step is to lead your low club. South will probably assume you are now leading low from J-x or from J-x-x. He can make sure of a club trick, in that case, by playing low again.

This allows East to win the second club trick with the jack. He returns a club to your ace, and you enjoy the sight of declarer's face as you defeat the contract.

79. A REVERSE FINESSE

According to the fortune-tellers, the four of clubs is a card of warning. If there is no four of clubs in your deck, you have a legitimate complaint.

West dealer
Neither side vulnerable

NORTH
♠ K Q 10 4
♡ J 3
♢ 7 5
♣ A Q 10 7 3

WEST
♠ 7 6 5
♡ A Q 5
♢ A K 9 8 3
♣ 6 4

EAST
♠ 2
♡ 10 8 6 4
♢ J 10 6 2
♣ K 9 8 5

SOUTH
♠ A J 9 8 3
♡ K 9 7 2
♢ Q 4
♣ J 2

West	North	East	South
1 ◇	2 ♣	2 ◇	2 ♠
3 ◇	3 ♠	All Pass	

Opening lead — ◇ K

West opened the king of diamonds, continued with the ace, and then shifted to a spade. Declarer won in dummy with the king of spades, cashed the ace of clubs and then led a low club from dummy.

East assumed that South was going to ruff, so he played low. (It would be foolish to play the king if South actually had no more.) South won the trick with the jack of clubs and returned a low heart. He could well afford to give up two hearts since he was not going to lose a club trick.

Strange Play

What was the explanation of South's strange play in clubs? Why didn't he take the normal finesse?

South reasoned that he could afford to lose a club trick to *West*, but not to East. If East won a club, he would return a heart, and this might enable the opponents to take two hearts and defeat the contract at once. If *West* won a club trick, however, he could take only *one* heart trick; after that dummy's clubs would be ready for discards.

The best chance to stop East from winning a club trick was to act like a man with a singleton deuce. As we have seen, this maneuver swindled East out of his club trick.

Well, then, what was all this hullabaloo about the four of clubs? Very simple: it didn't appear on the first club trick. When dummy's ace of clubs was led, West carefully played the six of clubs to begin a high-low.

If East had looked at the trick carefully, he would have seen the absence of the four of clubs staring him in the face. Who could have the missing card? If South had it, he would have taken the normal club finesse. If West had it, his play of the six of clubs was an obvious doubleton signal.

In short, the four of clubs is a card of warning *even when it isn't played*—provided that you're alert enough to be looking for it.

80. REMEMBER OLD TRAPS

The veteran bridge expert has a collection of old gags and traps, and he is not ashamed to trot them out when the wind seems to be blowing from the right direction.

South dealer
North-South vulnerable

NORTH
- ♠ J 4 2
- ♡ 9 5
- ◇ A Q 6 4
- ♣ A J 4 2

WEST
- ♠ A 8 5 3
- ♡ J 8 7 3
- ◇ 9 7 2
- ♣ 10 7

EAST
- ♠ 9 6
- ♡ A K 6 2
- ◇ J 10 8 3
- ♣ 9 6 5

SOUTH
- ♠ K Q 10 7
- ♡ Q 10 4
- ◇ K 5
- ♣ K Q 8 3

South	West	North	East
1 ♣	Pass	1 ◇	Pass
1 ♠	Pass	3 ♣	Pass
3 NT	All Pass		

Opening lead — ♡ 3

What would happen to this hand in the average game? East would conscientiously win the first trick with the king of hearts. Then he would take the ace of hearts and lead a third heart.

South would lose a spade and three hearts and would therefore score game and rubber. All very cut and dried. Probably nobody would see that opportunity had knocked while East had his hearing aid turned off.

Just put a veteran expert in the East seat, and things work out quite differently.

Recognizes Situation

The oldtimer in the East seat recognizes the heart situation. "Plot No. 179-A," he thinks to himself. "It's corny, but what can I lose?"

So East wins the first trick with the ace of hearts. The idea is to give South the impression that West has the king of hearts.

Now East leads the deuce of hearts instead of cashing his other top heart. If South is convinced that West has the king of hearts, he will finesse the ten of hearts at the second trick. South's only chance, or so he is led to believe, is that East has the jack of hearts.

If South finesses the ten of hearts in this hand, West wins with the jack. West leads a third heart to the king, and South turns purple as he realizes what has been done to him. The defenders take four hearts and the ace of spades, and then maintain a tactful silence while North moans bitterly.

Take a good look at East's hearts to recognize the plot the next time it comes along. You need A-K-x-x and your partner's lead must convince you that declarer has three cards in the suit. (You wouldn't want to lose the second trick to a *doubleton* queen.) Win the first trick with the ace, return a low card, and wear a bland, untroubled look.

BIDDING POINTERS

People often ask whether it pays to be aggressive in bidding. The answer depends on how well you play.

If you play the cards poorly, read one of my books on play and be sure to read my daily column each and every day. If possible, play in a few duplicate tournaments to widen the circle of players from whom you can learn new tricks.

While this is going on, keep your bidding horns pulled in. Start to bid more freely when you can come close to getting the most out of the cards.

When you feel that you can do pretty well in the play, make up your mind to bid a lot. Fortune favors the bold—in bridge as elsewhere.

In the average game, a good declarer has an advantage of about one trick per hand. He will gain, or the defense will throw away, about one trick per hand in contracts of game or lower.

You can't count on the opponents to give you a trick per hand at slam contracts. They have less chance for mistakes when they need only two tricks to defeat your contract.

Competitive Bidding

Make it a habit to compete savagely with your opponents. This is particularly true when your opponents are reluctant to double for penalties.

It's very comfortable to play against opponents who never step into the auction with doubt-ful values. You can open light, raise light, and steal hands that "belong" to the opponents. You'll either make these scratchy contracts or go down a trick or so—a small price to pay when the opponents have the values for a score of their own.

Learn the distinction between hands on which you must boost and those on which you must not. Hands No. 81 and 82 will illustrate the point.

When the opponents have found a good suit fit, they will usually try for game with 22 points or more in high cards. If they fail to make a move towards game, the chances are very good that they have fewer than 22 points—which means that you and your partner have roughly half the strength of the deck between you.

Moreover, when the opponents have a fit, the odds are very high that your side has a good fit in another suit. In short, you can rely on a good fit and roughly half the deck. You will not be hurt if you make a boosting bid.

There is no such safety when the opponents fail to discover a fit. If they have a misfit, your side may have a similar misfit. Moreover, they may stop short for lack of a fit. They may have more than 22 points between them, which means that your side may have only about 16 or 17 points. You may be hurt badly if you try a boosting bid without either a fit or adequate strength.

Strong Trumps

A strong trump suit is both a sword and a shield. In competitive situations bid one trick more when you have a powerful trump suit rather than let the opponents buy the hand.

If you become declarer, your trumps will protect you from disaster even though you may not make your contract. What's more, the opponents may discard badly and give you a trick or two when you run your long trump suit.

Bid conservatively when you have a broken trump suit. You will learn about astronomical numbers—such as 1100, 1400, 1700, and so on—when you run into a bad trump break with a doubtful trump suit.

Deliberate Overbidding

We all know games in which it is considered impolite to double for penalties or to overbid deliberately. We live in a big world, and people are entitled to have the sort of bridge game that pleases them.

If you play in a game of that sort, go along with them. Bid decorously and don't double anybody.

But if you play in a less namby-pamby game, you must expect to be doubled when you overbid. This shouldn't stop you from overbidding, for deliberate overbidding is one of the marks of the expert.

Remember that the value of a part score is about 150 points and that a game is worth about 500 points, all told. You can afford to overbid and let the opponents take their points in the form of penalties instead of scores below the line.

One of the advantages of good sacrifice bidding is that you may dish the opponents out of a game for a small penalty. Another is that you may push the opponents beyond their depth and thus turn a loss into a profit. Still a third is that you may find yourself making your sacrifice bid, particularly when the opponents are weak defenders.

Study Hands 92, 93, and 94 to see how sacrifice bids should be undertaken. When your hand is clearly worth a sacrifice, make your maximum bid all in one jump. Don't bid gradually, allowing the opponents to exchange information in the meantime. You are far more likely to push an opponent overboard with a fast sacrifice than if you get there gradually.

The time for a gradual sacrifice is when you want to be coaxed up. If you know what you're doing, you have a good hand and are trying to get doubled.

Don't let your opponents play the hand at a comfortable low contract when they have discovered a fit. Boost them one trick higher, and you'll often show a profit instead of a loss.

South dealer
North-South vulnerable

NORTH
♠ Q 10 9 5
♡ A 10 4
◇ 9 3
♣ Q 6 4 2

WEST	EAST
♠ A 6 2	♠ K J 8 4
♡ 6 5 2	♡ 8
◇ 10 5 4	◇ K J 8 7 6 2
♣ A K J 7	♣ 9 3

SOUTH
♠ 7 3
♡ K Q J 9 7 3
◇ A Q
♣ 10 8 5

South	West	North	East
1 ♡	Pass	2 ♡	Pass
Pass	Double	Pass	3 ◇
Pass	Pass	3 ♡	Pass
Pass	Pass		

Opening lead — ♣ K

It wasn't safe for West to overcall at his first turn. His hand was weak and his distribution was balanced, which meant that he might be slaughtered if he stepped into the auction.

The situation was different at West's next turn. North and South would have gone on with substantially more than half of the high cards in the deck. Hence their decision to stop meant that East and West held close to half of the strength. Moreover, the fit in hearts for North-South virtually guaranteed a fit in some other suit for East-West.

For these reasons, West reopened the auction by doubling two hearts. This was a take-out double, asking East to bid his best suit.

One Too High

East obliged, and South was pushed up to three hearts. This was just one trick too high.

West opened the king of clubs, and East signaled for a continuation by playing the nine. West followed with the ace of clubs and then led the jack of clubs.

Dummy had to put up the queen, and East ruffed with his singleton trump. The defenders then took their two spade tricks, defeating the contract.

If South had been allowed to play the hand at two hearts, he would have made his contract. The difference between making a good part score and going down one when vulnerable comes to more than 200 points, an amount worth consideration.

Incidentally, West should not bid four diamonds in this sort of hand even though he might occasionally make this contract. The idea is to boost the opponents, not to get stuck with the contract yourself.

When the opponents discover a fitting suit and stop short, you can afford to get into the auction and push them one trick higher. When they stop short without discovering a fit, don't try to push them. They may turn and bite.

West dealer
North-South vulnerable

NORTH
♠ J 10 5
♡ 10 9 6
♦ 9 6 5 4 3
♣ A 4

WEST	EAST
♠ A K 6 4	♠ 7 3 2
♡ A Q 5 2	♡ 8 4 3
♦ 7	♦ A J 10 8 2
♣ Q 9 8 3	♣ K 5

SOUTH
♠ Q 9 8
♡ K J 7
♦ K Q
♣ J 10 7 6 2

West	North	East	South
1 ♣	Pass	1 ♦	Pass
1 ♠	Pass	Pass	1 NT
Pass	Pass	Dbl.	All Pass

Opening lead — ♡ 2

South, one of the best players in the country, was competing in the finals of a national team championship. He hated to sell out to one spade, so he stepped bravely into the breach. It cost him 1100 points to stop the opponents from making a part score!

West opened the deuce of hearts, and South won with the

jack. For lack of anything better to do, he led a club to the ace and returned a low club.

East took the king of clubs and returned a heart. Declarer played low, and West won with the queen.

West next led a low spade, and South won with the eight. Declarer felt encouraged by the way things were developing. He had already taken three tricks, he still had a stopper in diamonds, and the opponents seemed to be fumbling.

Roof Falls In

South boldly led the jack of clubs, and the roof fell in. West took the queen of clubs and at last proceeded to cash his tricks.

West began by taking the top spades. This set up his last spade, so he took that also. East discarded a heart, and South discarded a low club.

West now knew that the hearts were going to break. He cashed the ace of hearts and his low heart.

The last heart was a crusher for poor South. He held the ten of clubs and his two diamonds, and had to part with one card. If he released the ten of clubs, West would cash the nine of clubs; and if South threw a diamond, West would lead a diamond and East would take the last two tricks.

Either way, South was sure to go down four tricks. "Very remarkable," South said, a sportsman to the end, "a squeeze against declarer!"

83. NOTRUMP MAY BE DANGEROUS

When you open the bidding because of your high cards it's all right to wander into a notrump contract. But when you have been persuaded to open partly by your unbalanced distribution, avoid notrump—especially if doubled by an opponent.

North dealer
North-South vulnerable

NORTH
♠ K 10 8 5 2
♡ 7
♢ K Q 6
♣ A J 7 3

WEST
♠ 6 3
♡ A Q J 9 8 3 2
♢ A J
♣ 8 4

EAST
♠ A Q J 9
♡ 10 5
♢ 8 7 3 2
♣ 9 6 2

SOUTH
♠ 7 4
♡ K 6 4
♢ 10 9 5 4
♣ K Q 10 5

North	East	South	West
1 ♠	Pass	1 NT	Double
All Pass			

Opening lead — ♠ 6

North had 13 points in high cards but no suit of any merit. It was his singleton that persuaded him to open the bidding; and that same singleton should have steered him away from notrump.

Poor South had no premoni-

tion of what was going to happen to him. He had a perfectly reasonable response of one notrump, but the innocent sometimes suffer with the guilty.

West opened the six of spades, and East won with the nine. He returned the ten of hearts, and West rattled off seven heart tricks.

Dummy could afford only one spade discard, so parted with one diamond and all four clubs. This brought dummy down to three spades and two diamonds by the time West had finished with the hearts.

West led another spade to give his partner a finesse. East returned a diamond, and West took the ace of diamonds and gave dummy a diamond trick. Dummy then had to give East the last two spade tricks.

Declarer's only trick was dummy's king of diamonds. He was down six, for a loss of 1,700 points!

Correct Bidding

Mind you, North shouldn't expect a major disaster at notrump, but he should be worried. Instead of staying in one notrump doubled, North should bid two clubs.

Nothing dramatic could happen to two clubs. As a matter of fact, West would bid his hearts and would probably wind up at a part score in hearts. Even if West got to game, his score would be nothing remotely like 1,700 points.

84. WHEN NOT TO OVERCALL

A flimsy overcall is the most dangerous bid in bridge. It is easier for an opponent to double for penalties than if you had made a flimsy opening bid.

West dealer
Both sides vulnerable

NORTH
♠ 10 7 5
♡ Q 10 8 5
♢ 10 8 7 5 4
♣ 2

WEST	EAST
♠ Q	♠ A K J 2
♡ A 7 2	♡ J 6 4 3
♢ A J 9 3	♢ K Q 2
♣ J 8 6 5 4	♣ 10 3

SOUTH
♠ 9 8 6 4 3
♡ K 9
♢ 6
♣ A K Q 9 7

West	North	East	South
Pass	Pass	1 ♠	2 ♣
Double	Pass	Pass	Pass

Opening lead — ♠ Q

South's overcall of two clubs practically begged for the ax, and the request was not denied. West had no trouble in pronouncing the word "Double," and South had his chance to show how well he could play a hopeless contract.

South didn't show any great enthusiasm for this opportunity. He managed to make three top trumps, one heart, and a low trump, for a total of five tricks. This was a praiseworthy effort, but it fell three tricks short of the contract, and the opponents scored 800 points in penalties.

What was wrong with the overcall? South had high cards enough and his distribution was unbalanced enough. What's more, his club suit was strong enough for an overcall.

Fatal Defect

The fatal defect was that South had too many losing cards in an opponent's strong suit. It was bad enough to have five low spades, as South discovered in the play of the cards. It was even worse that West was surely short in spades and would surely be itching for a chance to double any bid that South made.

This fact should lead to a general rule: Don't make a doubtful overcall when you have length in the opponent's bid suit.

Incidentally, if you think that no good player would dream of bidding two clubs on the South hand, there's some news in store for you. The hand was dealt in the 1957 European Championships, and at both tables the South player bid two clubs. One of them went for a ride of 800 points, as reported. The other South player escaped this harsh fate: His partner "rescued" at two diamonds and went for a ride of 1,100 points!

It is easier to punish the opponents at low contracts than at high bids. Sensible opponents will seldom get up high unless their own cards and partner's bidding promise reasonable safety.

East dealer
North-South vulnerable

NORTH
♠ Q 10 9 4
♡ 10 9 8 3
◇ 9 4
♣ J 10 9

WEST	EAST
♠ 6 2	♠ A K J 7 3
♡ K 7 2	♡ Q J 6 4
◇ K J 10 6	◇ 3 2
♣ K 8 5 2	♣ A 6

SOUTH
♠ 8 5
♡ A 5
◇ A Q 8 7 5
♣ Q 7 4 3

East	South	West	North
1 ♠	2 ◇	Double	All Pass

Opening lead — ♠ 6

South's overcall is very foolish and deserves to be punished. He has 12 high-card points and should pass all 12 of them. The test of an overcall is not how many points you have but how strong your suit is.

West's double shows some strength in diamonds, and some general strength elsewhere. If the opponents run to a different suit, West will be ready to double again; and if East bids a

new suit, West will not be dismayed.

Let's be more specific about what West promises with his double: Three or more probable defensive tricks, including either a sure trump trick or good prospects of a trump trick. In this case, West hopes to win three trump tricks and at least one of his side kings. West would not double if his only tricks were in diamonds.

North has no place to go, and East has cards that should be useful in the defense against diamonds. East would tend to take out the double if he had unusual length in his own suit or unusual shortness in the doubled suit.

Horrible Fate

South suffers a horrible fate at his contract of two diamonds doubled. East wins the first trick with the jack of spades and leads the ace of clubs. West signals encouragement with the eight of clubs and East continues with a club to the king and a club ruff.

The defenders eventually get another spade, a heart and three trump tricks without any great trouble. They win a total of nine tricks, collecting a penalty of 1,100 points.

If South passed instead of bidding two diamonds, West might get to three notrump and make it. He might even miss the game. The game is worth less than 500 points, so South's overcall costs at least 600 points.

The reports of insurance companies tell us that the bathtub is the most dangerous spot in a house. Stay out of bathtubs if you want to live a long, if solitary, life. On the same principle, never make a defensive overcall.

East dealer
Both sides vulnerable

NORTH
♠ 10 9 5 4
♡ 10 8 7 6 2
♢ 5 3
♣ Q J

WEST
♠ 6
♡ A Q J 4
♢ J 7 4
♣ K 8 7 5 2

EAST
♠ A Q J 7 3 2
♡ 9 3
♢ A 6
♣ A 6 3

SOUTH
♠ K 8
♡ K 5
♢ K Q 10 9 8 2
♣ 10 9 4

East	South	West	North
1 ♠	2 ♢	Double	All Pass

Opening lead — ♠ 6

Only a very fine player would double with the West cards. This sort of double should show prospects of a trump trick, shortness in partner's suit, and at least two defensive tricks outside of the doubled suit.

West hoped to pick up the value of a part score or of a game by his double, but he got far more than he hoped for.

West opened the six of spades, which East recognized immediately as a singleton. East won with the ace of spades but was in no hurry to give his partner the ruff. Since East had the ace of trumps the ruff couldn't run away.

East returned the nine of hearts, and West took the ace and queen. West continued with the jack of hearts, and East discarded a club.

Leads Trumps

South ruffed and led the king of diamonds, hoping to draw trumps quickly. East won with the ace of diamonds and led the deuce of spades to give West his ruff at last.

This called for a club return, since East would have led a higher spade to ask for a return in the higher side suit (hearts). West ruffed the deuce of spades with the seven of diamonds and led a club to the ace.

East returned a club to the king and ruffed a third round of clubs with the six of diamonds. Now East led a spade, and West's jack of diamonds could not be shut out.

After the defenders had finished picking South's bones clean, declarer could make only four tricks. The penalty of 1,100 points was ample compensation to West for the game he probably would not have bid.

Your partner's penalty doubles are suggestions, not commands. Here's a case in which the opening bidder should use his own judgment.

South dealer
East-West vulnerable

NORTH
♠ 7 3
♡ A Q 6 3
◇ J 7 4
♣ K J 6 5

WEST
♠ 6 2
♡ 10 5
◇ A K Q 10 9 5
♣ 8 4 3

EAST
♠ K 10 9 4
♡ 9 8 2
◇ 8 6 2
♣ Q 10 9

SOUTH
♠ A Q J 8 5
♡ K J 7 4
◇ 3
♣ A 7 2

South	West	North	East
1 ♠	2 ◇	Double	Pass
2 ♡	Pass	4 ♡	All Pass

Opening lead — ◇ K

South has a sound opening bid, and West has a fair overcall of two diamonds. North's double shows a good defensive hand but doesn't guarantee murderous strength in the enemy's suit.

South would be delighted to accept a double of two clubs or two hearts, but he is not eager to defend against two diamonds. Therefore he takes the double out by showing his second suit.

North is delighted to raise to four hearts. He knows that South has at most one diamond, so that his own strength in clubs is sure to be useful. If South has an opening bid with biddable spades and hearts and a singleton diamond he is sure to have a fine play for game in hearts.

Play Is Simple

The play at four hearts is simple, for South should make 10 or 11 tricks no matter how he goes at it. South's best plan is to ruff the second diamond and lead a low club to finesse dummy's jack at once. South cannot tell which finesse will work but should plan to try both.

East wins and probably returns a diamond for South to ruff. Declarer then cashes his two trumps, enters dummy with a club to draw the last trump, and tries the spade finesse. The rest is easy.

The basic bidding principle is very simple: The double of a low contract shows general strength and invites partner to co-operate in the defense. As I pointed out in another book: "If he has a good reason, an expert takes out a double just as though partner had shown his strength by a bid. And the doubler, if he is likewise an expert, not only expects this treatment but scolds his partner for letting the double stand if his hand clearly called for a take-out."

88. DON'T BE TRIGGER-HAPPY

Most good bridge players are enterprising doublers, but when you push enterprise too far, you usually wind up without your shirt.

East dealer
Neither side vulnerable

NORTH
♠ 7 6
♡ J 10 7 6
◇ A 2
♣ A J 9 6 2

WEST
♠ A 10 8 3
♡ 9 5
◇ K 7 6
♣ Q 8 7 5

EAST
♠ 4 2
♡ A K Q 8 4 2
◇ Q 8 5
♣ 10 4

SOUTH
♠ K Q J 9 5
♡ 3
◇ J 10 9 4 3
♣ K 3

East	South	West	North
1 ♡	2 ♠	Double	Pass
Pass	Pass		

Opening lead — ♡ 9

West had a good double of *four* spades, but no double at all of *two* spades. If West had passed, East would have been happy to pass likewise. If East had held more than a border-line opening bid, however, East would have acted when two spades was passed around to him. In other words, it wasn't necessary for West to bid his partner's cards; East was big enough to do his own work.

West opened the nine of hearts, dummy covered with the ten, and East won with the queen. East naturally supposed that his partner had the single-ton, rather than South. East therefore led the king of hearts next.

South ruffed, led a diamond to the ace, and returned a dia-mond. East played low, and West won with the king.

What was West to do now? For lack of anything better, West led a low club. Dummy's nine was covered by the ten, and South won with the king.

South ruffed a diamond in dummy, clearing the suit, and returned a trump. West cap-tured the king with the ace of spades and led another club.

Goes for Overtrick

By this time the entire hand was an open book to South. West had clearly started with only two hearts and exactly three diamonds. The double marked him with four spades, and West needed four clubs to the queen to have even a poor double.

Hence declarer finessed the jack of clubs, ruffed a low club, cashed the top trumps, and led a good diamond. West had to ruff, but then dummy's ace of clubs took the last trick, and South made an overtrick.

Instead of making a part score, South scored a game and 150 points in bonuses.

89. WHEN NOT TO DOUBLE

It's very foolish to double the opponents at the only low contract you can beat. Somebody takes that sort of double out, and then the bidding may get out of control.

```
            West dealer
       North-South vulnerable
              NORTH
              ♠ 8
              ♡ A 5
              ◇ A Q 8 7 5 2
              ♣ Q 7 4 3
WEST                      EAST
♠ A K J 7 3               ♠ 6 5 2
♡ Q J 6 4                 ♡ 10 9 8 7 2
◇ 3                       ◇ K J 10 9 6
♣ A K 5                   ♣ None
              SOUTH
              ♠ Q 10 9 4
              ♡ K 3
              ◇ 4
              ♣ J 10 9 8 6 2
```

West	North	East	South
1 ♠	2 ◇	Double	3 ♣
Double	All Pass		

Opening lead — ♣ K

East's double of two diamonds is foolish. South runs desperately from the double; and if South didn't, West would.

West is delighted to double three clubs, and now East doesn't know what to do. He doesn't enjoy passing, but he can't think of any good bid.

Makes Contract

South makes three clubs doubled, scoring game and rubber,
even if West adopts the correct defense of leading out three rounds of trumps. Declarer wins the third trump with dummy's queen and lets the eight of spades ride.

West takes the jack of spades and returns some red card. South gets to his hand with the king of hearts and leads the queen of spades to ruff out West's king. Now South can give up one spade trick and make his last spade.

Declarer wins four trumps, one ruff in dummy, one spade trick and the three top tricks in the red suits.

Even if South went down one trick it would be no triumph for East and West. They would be much better off if they bid and made their laydown game in hearts.

Let's suppose the bidding goes sensibly: East passes over two diamonds, and South also passes (not wanting to scream before he's hurt). West reopens with a takeout double, asking East to bid his best suit.

East naturally passes for penalties. If South also passes, North will go for the expected ride; East loses nothing by exercising restraint on the first round of bidding.

If South runs out of the double, East can safely bid three hearts at his next turn. He knows his partner has general strength. West will raise to four hearts, and East will make the game.

Even the best players occasionally flounder around in the bidding of a misfit hand. You can tell they're in trouble just by listening to the bidding, without even looking at anybody's cards. As an opponent, don't miss such an opportunity.

South dealer
Both sides vulnerable

NORTH
♠ A 7 2
♡ 4 3
♢ K Q 10 8 6
♣ 7 4 2

WEST
♠ K Q J 5
♡ K J 9 5
♢ 7 5 4 3
♣ 5

EAST
♠ 8 6
♡ 6 2
♢ A J 9 2
♣ K Q 8 6 3

SOUTH
♠ 10 9 4 3
♡ A Q 10 8 7
♢ None
♣ A J 10 9

South	West	North	East
1 ♡	Pass	2 ♢	Pass
2 ♡	Pass	2 NT	Pass
3 ♣	Pass	3 ♢	Pass
3 ♡	Pass	Pass	Double
Pass	Pass	Pass	

Opening lead — ♠ K

In this hand, East listened to the misery and waited patiently for the opponents to dig themselves in as deep as possible. Finally, when the last bid died away on the tortured air, East doubled.

Mind you, East didn't have a sound double of three hearts. He merely knew that the opponents needed good breaks to make their contract, and he could tell from his hand that they were going to get bad breaks. That justified his double.

East would not have doubled if he had held three hearts to the king and three small diamonds, together with other values. He would then know that South was going to get good breaks.

When the opponents are in obvious misery, you don't double just because you have strength. You double when you know that suits will break badly for declarer.

Double Is Very Productive

East's double worked like magic. Declarer took the first trick in dummy with the ace of spades and finessed the ten of hearts to West's jack. West continued spades, and East eventually overruffed dummy on the fourth round of the suit.

East next led a low club, and South finessed the nine. Declarer then led out the ace of hearts, still thinking that *East* had trump length. Now in serious trouble, he tried to cash the ace of clubs. West ruffed, cashed the king of hearts, and led a diamond. South still had two losing clubs, and made only five tricks.

The penalty was 1,100, or 700 points more than East would have scored if he had passed.

A certain kind of poker player (may his tribe increase) cannot be bluffed. No matter how many chips it may cost him, he will keep the game "honest." In a bridge game, the same kind of player cannot be shut out of the bidding.

East dealer
Both sides vulnerable

NORTH
♠ Q 9
♡ 10 9 4 3
♢ 4
♣ A K 10 7 6 2

WEST
♠ A K 10 8 6 4 3
♡ A 5
♢ J 6
♣ J 4

EAST
♠ 5
♡ K Q 8 2
♢ K 8 7
♣ Q 9 8 5 3

SOUTH
♠ J 7 2
♡ J 7 6
♢ A Q 10 9 5 3 2
♣ None

East	South	West	North
Pass	Pass	4 ♠	Pass
Pass	5 ♢	Pass	Pass
Double	All Pass		

Opening lead — ♠ K

West would not have opened with four spades in first or second position. In third position, since his partner had already passed, he could bid the game without fear of missing a slam.

Mind you, the fear of missing a slam is not the only restraint

on a bid of four spades. West could have gone for an 800-point ride if his opponents had taken time out for lunch. They would take two clubs and two diamonds, and then a third round of diamonds would assure two trump tricks.

In short, West's opening bid of four spades would be horrible in first or second position and dreadful in any other position. The only excuse for the bid was that West knew his customers. He knew South hated to be shut out.

Acts in Character

South acted in character when his turn came. His hand hadn't been worth a bid of one diamond to start with, but he blithely bid five diamonds when West tried to shut him out. East applied a penalty double, and the massacre was on.

West opened the king of spades, shifted to the ace of hearts, but shifted back to spades when East played the discouraging deuce of hearts. East ruffed the third spade, cashed the king and queen of hearts, and led a fourth heart. South ruffed with the ten of diamonds, and West over-ruffed. East still had to get a trick with the king of diamonds, so South was down 1,700 points.

The moral is very clear: Let the opponents steal something now and then. A policeman's lot is not a happy one.

92. SACRIFICE QUICKLY

Making a sacrifice bid is something like snuffing out a candle. If you try to do it slowly, you burn your fingers.

South dealer
North-South vulnerable

NORTH
♠ A 4
♡ Q 8 3
♢ Q 8 6 3
♣ 10 8 6 3

WEST
♠ K J 7 6 3
♡ J 9
♢ J 5
♣ A K 5 2

EAST
♠ Q 10 9 8 5 2
♡ 6 2
♢ 10 9 2
♣ Q J

SOUTH
♠ None
♡ A K 10 7 5 4
♢ A K 7 4
♣ 9 7 4

South	West	North	East
1 ♡	1 ♠	2 ♡	4 ♠
5 ♡	All Pass		

Opening lead — ♣ K

When this hand was played in a recent team match, the East cards were held at two different tables. Both players sacrificed at four spades, but only one of them burned his fingers.

At the first table, East jumped right to four spades. He knew that he was going to sacrifice sooner or later, and he saw no virtue in beating about the bush.

The immediate jump to four spades gave South a problem. He knew, of course, what East was doing, but he wasn't satisfied to accept a small penalty. After some inner debate South decided to take the boost to five hearts.

South was unlucky to find the wrong cards in his partner's hand. North had a useless ace and only low cards in clubs. West took two top clubs and led a third club for his partner to ruff. Down one.

Exchange of Information

At the other table East's gradual method of sacrificing allowed an exchange of information between South and North. This was bad for East and good for South.

East bid only two spades at his first turn. South promptly jumped to four hearts, showing his strength. East then woke up to the fact that he had to bid four spades.

Now, however, South could afford to pass. He had already indicated the nature of his hand and could allow North to make a decision. If North had values in the unbid suits, he could bid on to five hearts; if he had values in spades, he could double.

As it happened, an important part of North's hand was the ace of spades. It was a sure trick on defense but might be useless for offense. For this reason North doubled four spades.

West was down two, for a loss of 300 points. This was, of course, better than allowing South to score a vulnerable game but it was 400 points worse than pushing South overboard at five hearts.

93. SACRIFICE WITH GOOD DISTRIBUTION

Some hands are interesting not only for what happens but also for what doesn't happen. Sins of omission are less noticeable than those of commission, but they may be just as costly.

South dealer
Neither side vulnerable

NORTH
- ♠ 6 5 3 2
- ♡ Q 10 7 6 4 3
- ◇ 8 4
- ♣ A

WEST
- ♠ Q 10 9 8
- ♡ 5
- ◇ A K 5 2
- ♣ K Q J 5

EAST
- ♠ 7
- ♡ 9
- ◇ 10 9 7 6 3
- ♣ 10 9 8 6 4 2

SOUTH
- ♠ A K J 4
- ♡ A K J 8 2
- ◇ Q J
- ♣ 7 3

South	West	North	East
1 ♡	Double	4 ♡	All Pass

Opening lead — ◇ K

West took two top diamonds and then shifted to a club. Declarer took the ace of clubs, drew a trump, cashed the ace of spades, and ruffed a club to reach dummy.

He then led another spade from dummy. East discarded, and South played low, allowing West to win the trick.

Now West was caught in an end play. If he returned a spade, South would make both the king and the jack; if West returned anything else, dummy would ruff while South discarded the jack of spades.

What Was Wrong

There was nothing wrong with the way South played the hand—except that he should have been defending instead of playing the dummy. Or perhaps he should have been going down at a contract of *five* hearts.

East didn't have an ace or a face card, *but he should have sacrificed at five of a minor suit.* His magnificent distribution would have saved him from a severe penalty. East would be down only one trick at five of either minor suit.

There was no need for East to pick the suit himself, although a bid of five clubs could not be censured. East could, instead, bid four notrump over four hearts; and this would ask West to choose the minor suit.

This would be a dangerous bid to make with an inexperienced partner; a bid of five clubs would be safer. An expert partner would realize that East could not possibly want to play the hand at four notrump. Since East had bypassed spades, he clearly wanted to suggest five clubs or five diamonds as the final contract.

East would, of course, be better off losing 100 points than letting South make a game. And if North went on to five hearts, East would wind up with a profit on the hand.

94. LET YOURSELF BE COAXED

If you are old enough to remember when girls were shy young creatures, you should be able to bid freak hands well. The technique is to let yourself be coaxed into doing finally just what you always wanted to do.

South dealer
East-West vulnerable

NORTH
♠ 8 4 3
♡ J 10 5
♢ Q 5
♣ K 10 9 6 2

WEST
♠ A K Q 9 6 5
♡ A K 9 3
♢ 6
♣ Q 4

EAST
♠ J 7 2
♡ Q 8 7 6 4 2
♢ 8 4 3
♣ 5

SOUTH
♠ 10
♡ None
♢ A K J 10 9 7 2
♣ A J 8 7 3

South	West	North	East
1 ♢	Double	Pass	1 ♡
2 ♣	4 ♡	5 ♣	Pass
Pass	Double	Pass	5 ♡
6 ♣	Double	All Pass	

Opening lead — ♠ K

When this hand was played in a tournament recently, many players jumped to three clubs (or even higher) on the second round of bidding. This and the later bidding made it clear to West that South had outlandish distribution.

Several shrewd players sacrificed at six hearts with the West hand. This cost only 200 points, less than even a game, let alone a slam.

The sacrifice was hard to find when South bid his hand gradually. South should bid only two clubs at his second turn. The important thing to remember about freak hands is that at least one opponent usually has a freakish hand also. If you reveal your strength, one of the opponents will take fright and run into a safe suit of his own.

Sure Slam

When North raises to five clubs, South should feel sure of a slam at clubs. *Nevertheless, he must not bid the slam.* This would expose the situation to the opponents.

It sounds for all the world as though North has stabbed at a sacrifice against four hearts. In fact, North thinks that he is doing just that. South, although he knows better, must keep quiet. He must allow West to take action against five clubs.

South is rewarded for his patience when he gets the chance to bid six clubs. As expected, this contract is doubled and made. South scores more than a thousand points for his doubled slam instead of only 200 points against a sacrifice of six hearts.

When your partner opens with one notrump, your problem is whether to look for game in notrump or in a major suit. The problem is sometimes solved by bidding the opponent's suit.

South dealer
North-South vulnerable

NORTH
♠ K J 4 2
♡ A 6 5 4
◇ 6 3
♣ K 10 3

WEST
♠ 9 7 6
♡ Q 2
◇ K Q J 10 5 4
♣ A 5

EAST
♠ 10 5
♡ 10 9 8 3
◇ 7 2
♣ J 8 7 6 4

SOUTH
♠ A Q 8 3
♡ K J 7
◇ A 9 8
♣ Q 9 2

South	West	North	East
1 NT	2 ◇	3 ◇(!)	Pass
3 ♠	Pass	4 ♠	Pass
Pass	Pass		

Opening lead — ◇ K

If West had passed, North would have bid two clubs, the Stayman Convention. This would say nothing about clubs, but would ask South to show a major suit if he had one.

When West actually bid two diamonds, North could no longer make his conventional bid of two clubs. He got the same result by bidding three diamonds. This couldn't show

diamond strength, since North could show that by doubling. The bid was clearly meant as an invitation of some kind.

South was glad to show his major suit, whereupon North promptly raised to game. This got South to the best game contract.

West opened the king of diamonds, and South took the ace of diamonds and drew three rounds of trumps. Declarer then finessed the jack of hearts, losing to West's queen.

West cashed a diamond and led a third diamond, forcing dummy to ruff. Declarer next took the king and ace of hearts, hoping for a 3-3 break in the suit. When the suit failed to break, South had to guess who had the jack of clubs.

Counting Tells the Story

South could count out West's original hand. West had followed to two rounds of hearts and three rounds of trumps. West was also known to have started with exactly six diamonds, since East had followed to only two rounds of that suit. This left room for only two clubs in the West hand.

With five clubs in the East hand and only two clubs in the West, the odds were 5 to 2 that East held the jack. Declarer therefore led a low club from dummy and finessed the nine from his own hand.

West had to win with the ace of clubs, and South's game was then assured.

In certain hands, each side can do very well at its own best trump suit. If both sides enter the auction, there may be quite a struggle. The side that bids first has a big advantage because it may bluff the opponents right out.

South dealer
East-West vulnerable

NORTH
♠ 6
♡ 10 9 6 5
◊ A 10 8 7 3
♣ A 8 4

WEST
♠ K Q 7 3
♡ 3
◊ Q 9 6 2
♣ K 9 5 3

EAST
♠ A J 9 5 2
♡ A 7
◊ J 4
♣ Q J 7 2

SOUTH
♠ 10 8 4
♡ K Q J 8 4 2
◊ K 5
♣ 10 6

South	West	North	East
2 ♡	Pass	4 ♡	All Pass

Opening lead — ♠ K

South's opening bid of two hearts will seem strange to those who use standard bidding methods. The traditional two-bid shows tremendous strength; the "weak" two-bid shows only a strong suit in a hand that is almost, but not quite, worth a normal opening bid.

The weak opening bid allows North to steal the hand. North cannot be sure that his hand will give South a reasonable play for ten tricks, but he does know that South has very little defense against a spade contract. Since North likewise has little defense, he jumps to four hearts as a two-way proposition: partly to shut the opponents out and partly in the hope of making a game.

The jump bid has the desired effect. East is silenced. East may, of course, suspect that he is being jobbed—but how can he risk a bid at so high a level?

Game for Both Sides

South easily makes four hearts, losing only one spade, one heart, and one club. If East played the hand at four spades, however, he would score a game for *his* side, losing only two diamonds and one club.

Each side can make game at its own best trump suit.

If South uses traditional bidding methods, he must pass. West and North will likewise pass, and East will open the bidding with one spade. After this opening bid, South cannot steal the hand. West will get to four spades, and East may be allowed to play the hand there. At best, North and South may sacrifice by bidding five hearts, settling for a small loss.

Take a good look at the South hand if you like the idea of the weak two-bid. Such a bid should promise a strong six-card suit in a hand that is not quite worth a normal opening bid.

97. WHEN TO BE UNSCIENTIFIC

When you open with a "weak" two-bid, you hope to make life difficult for the opponents. You have only a strong suit in a hand that is not quite worth an opening bid. So far as you are concerned, the hand "belongs" to the opponents. Despite your modest intentions, your partner may leap violently to a very high contract.

South dealer
Both sides vulnerable

NORTH
♠ None
♡ A 9 8 4 3
♢ A K Q 7 6 3
♣ 8 5

WEST
♠ A 8 7 4
♡ 7
♢ J 10 8 5
♣ K 10 6 4

EAST
♠ Q J 10 9 5 3
♡ 10
♢ 2
♣ A Q J 7 2

SOUTH
♠ K 6 2
♡ K Q J 6 5 2
♢ 9 4
♣ 9 3

South	West	North	East
2 ♡	Pass	6 ♡	All Pass

Opening lead — ♠ A

South has a model hand for a weak two-bid in hearts. The hand is not quite worth a normal opening bid, but it is far from worthless.

The weak two-bid promises a strong six-card suit with very little outside strength—a king, or perhaps an ace. Partner should consider a game if he has a very fine distributional fit or if he has more than the values for a normal opening bid.

In this case North should consider a slam. South will easily win 12 tricks if he has a strong heart suit and either the king or ace of clubs.

Science vs. Larceny

A scientific North would do his best to find out whether or not South had club strength. He might do so by bidding diamonds, following with a cue-bid in spades, and then jumping to five hearts.

This would invite South to bid six hearts if he could take care of the unbid clubs. It would also invite the opponents to lead clubs.

A practical player should just leap to six hearts without any pretense at science. If West leads a diamond or a spade, the slam should be ice cold. Even if West leads a club, there may still be hope; South may have ace, king, or singleton. The odds are against finding club strength in the South hand, but the odds must be about 2 to 1 that West will lead the wrong suit.

98. THE BLACKWOOD CONVENTION

The Blackwood Convention supplies a simple way of finding out how many aces your partner has.

```
South dealer
Both sides vulnerable
            NORTH
            ♠ Q 10 5 2
            ♡ 8 3
            ◇ K Q 9
            ♣ A J 7 2
WEST                    EAST
♠ 6                     ♠ 9 4
♡ J 9 4 2               ♡ 10 6
◇ A 10 5 3             ◇ J 8 7 4 2
♣ 10 9 8 6             ♣ K Q 4 3
            SOUTH
            ♠ A K J 8 7 3
            ♡ A K Q 7 5
            ◇ 6
            ♣ 5
```

South	West	North	East
1 ♠	Pass	3 ♠	Pass
4 NT	Pass	5 ◇	Pass
6 ♠	All Pass		

Opening lead — ♣ 10

After North's jump to three spades, South is interested only in aces. South cannot make any slam at all if North is aceless; can make a small slam if North has one ace; and can make a grand slam if North has two aces.

South jumps to four notrump, the bid that begins the Blackwood Convention.

North must respond five clubs if he has no aces; five diamonds, if he has one ace; five hearts, if he has two aces; and so on.

In this case, North bids five diamonds to show one ace. South can see that one ace is missing, and he therefore bids six spades.

This bid silences North. South has all of the information and has made a final decision. North cannot go on to a grand slam (unless he hates his partner and wants to help the opponents).

There is nothing to the play. Declarer wins the first trick in dummy with the ace of clubs, draws two rounds of trumps, and then goes after the hearts. One small heart is ruffed in dummy, and then South has the rest of the tricks except for the ace of diamonds.

Asking for Kings

In this hand South is interested only in aces, but sometimes a player needs information about kings.

You find out about kings by bidding five notrump after you have received an answer to your bid of four notrump. Your bid of five notrump announces that no aces are missing; and it asks your partner to show by his response how many kings he holds.

Partner bids six clubs to show no kings; six diamonds, to show one king; and so on. The method is the same as in the responses to four notrump, except that the bids are one trick higher.

Experts use cue bids to check on slam possibilities largely because this permits both partners to use their judgment.

South dealer
Both sides vulnerable

NORTH
♠ K J 7 2
♡ 5 3
◇ K 6 4
♣ A K 6 3

WEST
♠ 9 4
♡ 10 9 8 6
◇ J 9 5 2
♣ J 9 8

EAST
♠ 6 3
♡ A 7 4 2
◇ 10 8 7
♣ Q 10 7 4

SOUTH
♠ A Q 10 8 5
♡ K Q J
◇ A Q 3
♣ 5 2

South	West	North	East
1 ♠	Pass	3 ♠	Pass
4 ◇	Pass	5 ♣	Pass
6 ♠	All Pass		

Opening lead — ♡ 10

After North's jump to three spades, South knows only that a slam is possible. It wouldn't help to find out how many aces are held by North. This is very often true when a player has a worthless doubleton in an unbid suit. The Blackwood Convention is of no use in such cases.

For example, assume that North has both of the missing aces, with three small diamonds. South must lose a club and at least one diamond, and no slam is therefore possible.

It is foolish to ask your partner how many aces he holds when you don't know what to do with the answer. Instead, therefore, South makes a cue bid and leaves the next move up to North.

How does North know that South is interested in a slam when he bids four diamonds? After a double raise in a major suit, any bid of a new suit must be a slam try. If South is interested only in game he simply bids four of his major or three notrump.

Responding to Cue Bids

As we have seen, the opening bidder shows an ace (usually his lowest ace) and an interest in slam by way of a cue bid. His partner responds in the same way. That is, the partner shows the cheapest ace if he is interested in a slam; otherwise, he signs off by returning to the agreed suit.

In this case, North is interested in a slam and shows the ace of clubs. Since this takes the partnership beyond the level of game, it is clear that North has very good values for his jump raise.

This is just what South needs to know. His partner has the ace of clubs and maximum values. South therefore jumps at once to six spades.

There is no problem in the play of the cards. The defenders can take the ace of hearts, but then South easily wins the rest.

It isn't easy to bid a good slam that depends largely on distribution instead of high cards.

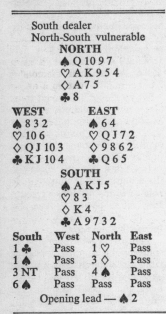

South dealer
North-South vulnerable

NORTH
♠ Q 10 9 7
♡ A K 9 5 4
♢ A 7 5
♣ 8

WEST
♠ 8 3 2
♡ 10 6
♢ Q J 10 3
♣ K J 10 4

EAST
♠ 6 4
♡ Q J 7 2
♢ 9 8 6 2
♣ Q 6 5

SOUTH
♠ A K J 5
♡ 8 3
♢ K 4
♣ A 9 7 3 2

South	West	North	East
1 ♣	Pass	1 ♡	Pass
1 ♠	Pass	3 ♢	Pass
3 NT	Pass	4 ♠	Pass
6 ♠	Pass	Pass	Pass

Opening lead — ♠ 2

In this hand North was only mildly interested when South opened with one club, since North's singleton in his partner's suit was not really an asset. When South bid spades, later on, North considered bidding toward a slam.

The question was whether the singleton club had become an asset after all. If South had several top clubs and rather weak spades, the slam would be a poor gamble. But if South had strong spades and weak clubs, the slam would be a very good bet. (There was no need to consider the possibility that South had great strength in both black suits, since then South would bid the slam without any particular urging by North.)

In a situation of this kind, North should not try to guess what his partner has. He should describe his hand and leave it to South to make the decision.

Jump Bid Significant

North shows his distribution by making a jump bid in a new suit and then raising spades. A player who bids three suits, with a jump bid at some stage, shows a singleton in the fourth suit. What's more, he guarantees the ace in the secondary side suit (diamonds in this case).

Given this information, South is eager to bid the slam in spades. He knows that his partner has a good heart suit, the ace of diamonds, excellent support for spades, and a singleton in clubs. What else does he need for slam?

There is no problem in the play of the cards. Dummy wins the first trick with the seven of spades, and declarer cashes the top hearts. When these get by, South ruffs a heart with the ace of trumps, enters dummy with the ace of diamonds, and ruffs another heart with the king of trumps. The jack of spades is led and overtaken in dummy, and trumps are drawn.

IMPERFECT HANDS

You are playing bridge at a friend's home, and everything is going normally. There is a faint whiff of coffee in the air, mingled with the aroma of your favorite cake. But you want to finish the rubber before taking time out, so somebody deals the next hand.

You pick up your cards, glance at them, and gulp. You have been dealt 13 spades!

What do you do?

Thank goodness you don't have a weak heart, but you almost faint with excitement anyway. You abandon the idea of bidding the hand normally. Instead, you show your cards face up.

"Call the newspaper," somebody urges. "They'll want to take a picture of this hand. They'll want to send a reporter over."

It Isn't News

Sadly enough, the newspaper isn't excited over your 13 spades. It isn't news. Maybe they'd send over a reporter if you were dealt 14 spades, but 13 is old stuff.

Now this is very peculiar. In the United States and Canada combined, according to the odds, somebody should get 13 cards of a suit about once every four years. Isn't it news when this unusual thing happens to

John Jones, right here in town?

It should be, perhaps, but actually about 20 times each year somebody is dealt 13 cards of a suit. So it isn't as unusual as you think.

What's more, about 19 times out of 20 that unusual hand is 13 spades.

Why should a hand come along about 80 times as often as you should expect? And why shouldn't the 13-card hand be in hearts, diamonds or clubs just as often as spades?

Nobody knows the answer to these questions. If you want to believe in leprechauns or gremlins, more power to you. As for myself, I prefer to believe in practical jokers.

The joker finds a chance to smuggle in a prepared deck when nobody is looking. He expects a lot of fun and excitement, but expects to have even more fun when he reveals the truth. But lucky John Jones takes his 13 spades so seriously that the joker doesn't dare upset the applecart. He is stuck with his gag, and so is everybody else.

So if you pick up 13 spades one of these fine evenings, it's all right to exult as though you were in Paradise—but look around carefully. There's probably a snake in your Garden of Eden.

WHAT EXPERTS SAY

The higher you climb in bridge circles, the couther the conversation. When you make a ghastly play, your partner doesn't call you a blithering idiot. "You're clearly doing your best," he will comment in a treacly tone; and the iron will enter into your soul.

When he gets a horrible score in a tournament, the expert calls it a "nice little game." Anything worse is a "gentleman's score."

When the expert is trapped into playing with a gentleman, does he later recount to his cronies all of the gentleman's misdeeds? Not at all. He gives credit where credit is due. "He played very well," the expert announces. "Revoked only once."

Proper Respect

The expert is very careful to pay proper respect to players of the female persuasion. If he knows her, the expert will refer to her by name. "Helen Sobel bid one spade," he will relate. Or "Edith Kemp led the eight of hearts."

If the expert doesn't know the female player, he is careful to call her a lady. For example, "A lady won the first trick with the king of diamonds."

I'll never forget the time my wife played in the Life Master Individual at a national tournament a couple of years ago. I wasn't playing in the event, and I strolled into the playing room and sat down at her table just in time to hear her bid a hand with an expert from the Midwest.

My wife opened the bidding with one heart, and her partner bid one notrump. My wife bid two hearts, and her partner bid two notrump. My wife bid three hearts, and her partner bid three notrump. Doubled, and down three. Three hearts was unbeatable.

Nobody said a word, and my wife moved on to her next table. The Midwesterner caught my eye and began to explain what had happened. "The lady bid one heart," he said.

I interrupted him indignantly. "That was no lady," I declared. "That was my wife."

PLAYING FOR EXTRA TRICKS

How hard should you try for an extra trick?

The answer depends on the contract, who is playing the hand, where the hand is being played, what risk is involved and a host of other factors.

Let's take a simple case. The contract is four spades with both sides vulnerable. The ques-

tion is whether or not to play for an overtrick.

Early in the evening, when everybody is quite fresh, you might spend a minute or two on the attempt to get 30 additional points. A couple of hours later, however, an opponent would bark bitterly: "We'll give you the 30 points if you're so hungry. Let's get on to the next hand."

This is especially true if you're playing the hand on a commuting train. You can get away with bad bidding or bad play or both in a commuters' game, but you can't get away with anything that wastes time.

Personalities alter cases. I played very little bridge during World War II; the government had other ideas about what I should be doing. But I did get into one game in New Delhi with a two-star general who liked to play for extra tricks. The next highest rank in the game was a mere lieutenant colonel. Nobody told the general to stop stalling.

The Question of Risk

If your attempt to snag an extra trick will jeopardize an otherwise sure contract, you have to be slightly crazy to play for the extra trick. The difference between making the game and going down one is 720 points. You can practically never afford to gamble 720 points in the attempt to gain a mere 30 points.

Suppose your play for the extra trick is safe unless each of four finesses loses. Now you know what you'd do if you took four finesses and lost each one of them. You'd be throwing things, and your partner would be muttering, and the opponents would be snickering. But this is only a 15 to 1 shot. When you gamble 720 points to pick up only 30 you need odds of 24 to 1 in your favor.

It's possible to work out hands in which this kind of risk is mathematically sound, but it isn't worth the trouble. It's simpler and very nearly exact to follow this conservative rule: Don't risk an otherwise guaranteed contract in the attempt to make an extra trick.

Tournaments Are Different

You can't apply this conservative rule in a tournament. If you fail to play for extra tricks in tournaments you'll make lots of friends—but none of them will be willing to take you on as a partner.

When you play a hand in a tournament at an unimportant contract, like two clubs, you struggle just as hard to make an extra trick as if you were trying to make the twelfth trick at a slam contract. There's no such thing as an unimportant contract in a tournament.

DON'T CHASE GOOD LUCK

The best way to improve your results at bridge is to take on more responsibility. If you blame yourself silently and thoughtfully for almost everything that goes wrong, you may be able to prevent things from going wrong the same way in the future.

Most people prefer to rely on magic. You probably know somebody who takes care not to walk on sidewalk cracks when he sets out to play bridge;

or somebody who knocks wood hastily if you call attention to his good luck. They believe in their personal luck, and they do these odd things to get the luck or stop it from leaving.

Others try to catch up with luck by noticing which way the cards are running. One day a wag printed this notice on the bulletin board of a famous bridge club: "Saturday, June 1st. Temperature 79. Cards running North-South, except at Table 4. Spades breaking badly. Conditions favorable for no-trump."

Most of the players in the club that day tried to sit North-South even though they knew the notice was a joke. Maybe there was something in it!

It's comforting to use this approach to bridge. If anything goes wrong, you don't have to work for better bidding or more accurate play; just try to plant

your seat the way the cards are running.

In the long run you have the same kind of cards no matter where you put your seat. You can do better with those cards by working with your head.

If you get a poor result with a hand, look for your mistakes in bidding or play. When your partner has made the mistake, try to recall whether you led him astray or whether you could have saved him. Even if your partner pulled the boner all by himself, perhaps you can find a sympathetic word to restore his morale.

You don't have to be a martyr or wear a hair shirt in your eagerness to take the responsibility for whatever goes wrong. It isn't even necessary to let anybody else know what you are doing. Just put the emphasis on improving your methods instead of chasing after good luck.

BRIDGE ETHICS

Poker players cannot understand bridge ethics. "If you're trying to make a monkey out of your opponent," says the poker player, "why can't you do a little acting?"

Take the situation where you have only one card of a suit. The poker player would like to study his hand when that suit is led, as though he had a problem. Perhaps he would even finger one or two other cards before extracting the card he must automatically play.

A bridge player would consider this unethical. He is will-

ing to deceive an opponent by the card he plays but not by the manner of playing the card.

Voice Control

Or take the question of voice control. The average beginner bids in a faint, fearful tone when he has a bad hand; in a loud, confident tone when he has a good hand.

A good bridge player tries to make all his bids in the same neutral tone. He blushes for shame if his emotions come to the surface while he is bidding.

Why is this so? Tradition.

Every game has its own traditions, but these may be stronger than laws. If you're playing baseball it's all right to steal a base; but if you're playing chess you don't try to snitch your opponent's king while he's looking the other way.

Code Varies

Your code of ethics in a bridge game depends partly on how good a player you are. The better you are, the stricter your code must be.

You expect a beginner to bid joyfully when he likes what is going on, but sadly when he sniffs trouble in the wind. Nobody has ever told the beginner this is improper. He might not believe you if you told him. And anyway, everybody in his game acts the same way.

More control is expected of a good player. Complete control is expected of an expert.

The idea is that you're trying to win by your skill in bidding and your skill in playing. Your skill in acting should not be a factor.

How strictly should you personally live up to the proper code of bridge ethics? Try to do better than the average level in your group of bridge players. Perhaps only a saint could live up to the highest possible standard. But most players are so thoughtless about ethics that you can put yourself on a much higher level with only a little effort.

BRIDGE PROBABILITIES

No matter how careful you are, sooner or later somebody will talk to you about probabilities and percentages. The only way to protect yourself is to know something about the subject so that you can talk faster and louder.

The first and most important rule of probability is to forget about it if you know something better. If an opponent drops the ace of spades on the floor, you don't need a slide rule to work out who has it.

The same principle applies when you have a clear inference from the bidding or early play. Use your knowledge of bridge and your knowledge of people rather than mere mathematics.

When you have nothing else to guide you, use probability. It's better than nothing.

Finesses

A finesse is an even chance. For example, suppose you must finesse for the king of trumps. There is a 50-50 chance the finesse will work.

If you take two finesses, the odds are 3 to 1 against being successful in both. If you need only one of those two finesses, the odds are 3 to 1 that one of them will work for you.

Suit Breaks

Sometimes you want to estimate how the missing cards of

a suit will be divided between the two opponents. You can't really prophesize; you can only estimate.

If three cards are missing, they will break 2–1 78 times out of 100. They will break 3–0 the remaining 22 times.

If five cards are missing, they will break 3–2 about 68 times out of 100. The other breaks are far less frequent.

Here is your rule for an *odd* number of cards: the most equal division is the most likely.

Now consider the even numbers.

When you are missing four cards, they will break 2–2 about 40 times out of 100. They will break 3–1 about 50 times.

When you are missing six cards, they will break 3–3 about 36 times out of 100. They will break 4–2 about 48 times.

Here is your rule for an *even* number of cards: the most equal division is not the most likely.

Remember the two short rules to guide you in actual play. If you like to know the figures, clip this article out and paste it inside one of your old hats. It may come in handy some day.

NEVER TRUST ANYBODY!

Every bridge player should know the story of the man who lifted his ten-year-old son to the top of a six-foot ladder and urged the boy to jump. "Don't be afraid," he coaxed, "I'll catch you."

The boy jumped, and the father stepped back and let him land on the floor.

"That's your first lesson," he told the howling lad. "Never trust anybody—not even your father."

Every good bridge teacher should install a tall ladder in his studio to teach this lesson. A painful tumble is a small price to pay for a valuable lesson.

The Fishbein Case

Consider the case of Harry Fishbein and the Famous Expert. During the past 25 years Fishbein has won practically

every bridge championship at some time or other, some of them more than once. He is even better known to his fellow experts for the bewildering variety of his berets (he has six closets full of them!) and for the equally bewildering nature of his speech (he uses words nobody ever heard of).

Fishbein, the principal ornament of New York's Mayfair Club, drops into the Cavendish Club occasionally to see how the other half lives. There he got into a game, not long ago, with a Famous Expert as his partner.

With both sides vulnerable, the player at Fishbein's left dealt and bid four spades. There were two passes, and it was up to Fishbein.

Fishbein had a wonderful hand. No spades at all, but top cards in each of the other suits. He was practically ready to guarantee a slam in any of the unbid suits. The trouble was that he didn't know which to bid.

Expert Bid

This is no great problem for an expert. There is a special expert bid that describes just this sort of hand. You bid four notrump, and your partner is supposed to take out in his longest suit. You might not use this bid with your Aunt Tillie, because she's old-fashioned, but you can use it with any really fine player.

Fishbein peered across the table over his bifocals. The Famous Expert was still sitting there, so Fishbein confidently bid four notrump. He could rely on his partner.

"Double," snapped the opponent. Once more there were two passes, and once more it was up to Fishbein.

Again this was no great problem. All you have to do with an expert partner is redouble, and he'll know that you're commanding him to name his longest suit. It's easy.

So Fishbein redoubled.

* * *

Remember that story about the tall ladder?

Everybody passed the redouble, and the opponents took the first ten spade tricks and then graciously gave Fishbein the last three. Down seven, vulnerable, redoubled, came to the tidy little sum of 4,000 points.

You already know the moral: Never trust anybody—not even your father!

THE WAR BETWEEN THE SEXES

"Something puzzles me about you bridge columnists," writes my old friend Constant Reader. (I can't tell you much about Constant except that he, or she, uses very delicate perfume on his notepaper and very nearly got me in Dutch with my wife.) "You always refer to your players as men," C.R. continues. "Don't you like girls enough to play bridge with them?"

What an odd idea! I am not now, nor have I ever been a girl hater—except for a brief interlude when I was busy deciding whether to be a great athlete or a fireman. Moreover, most of my bridge-playing friends believe in being kind to girls. You'd be surprised how much trouble this can cause.

Actually, Constant, old boy, I refer to a bridge player as "he" in an effort to be fair. It looks prejudiced if I write "*her* redouble cost 1,400 points" or "*her* play left something to be desired—namely six tricks."

Women Shine

People used to ask me whether men or women are the better bridge players. Women are better, except that men are best.

If you took all of the bridge players in the world and worked out a way to get an average figure for their skill, the women would be above that average and the men would be below.

There's a reason for the general superiority of the women. (If there weren't, the men would cook one up anyway.) They have more time than men, and many manage to get some practice in the afternoons. Practice makes less imperfect. Moreover, women tend to be more docile than men and therefore follow expert advice.

If you disregard average bridge players and concentrate only on experts, you find that the story is reversed. The men outshine the women.

I would explain this, if I were a woman, by pointing out that when a man gets interested in a game he goes completely overboard and wastes all his time and energy on it—which women are too sensible to do. The masculine explanation is that top-flight bridge calls for stamina, courage and aggressiveness—all qualities in which men tend to excel.

Pick your own explanation.

FALSE BRIDGE NOTIONS

Everybody knows what happens when bad money begins to circulate. People stow the good money under the mattress and keep passing the bad money around. The same rule seems to apply to true and false notions about bridge.

Several times a week, from widely separated parts of the continent, I get a question about responding to a forcing bid. "My partner bid two diamonds," writes a lady in Alberta, "and I kept it open by bidding two notrump. She bid three diamonds and I passed. I had a really terrible hand, so I didn't want to bid any more. The opponent said I just had to bid because that was one of the laws of the game. Is this a fact?"

No, it isn't a fact; but hundreds of very nice people think it is.

If you want to pass your partner's forcing bid you have a legal right to do so. It is often unwise to pass, but there is no law against being foolish.

The confusion arises because bridge authorities love to lay down "rules" for good bidding. These rules are usually very good advice, but they do not have the force of law.

Before the Lead

People often ask about putting the trumps down before the opening lead. Perhaps you've seen this done in a social game: the opening leader waits for the dummy to put down her trumps before the lead is made.

You will never see this in an expert game for the very simple reason that neither law nor custom has confirmed this practice.

Sometimes, when I tell people this they reply: "It may not be expert, but it's very polite, isn't it?" There's no answer to this question. Some people consider it impolite to double an opponent. They play a very polite game, but it isn't bridge.

The Blank Hand

One of the most persistent false notions about the game concerns the blank hand. "I was dealt a hand with neither an ace nor a face card," goes a typical complaint. "Do I have the right to ask for a new deal?"

Yes, indeed. You have the right to ask for a new deal and $20 in gold. But the opponents don't have to pay any attention to you.

You're entitled to sympathy when you get a really terrible hand. If you're nice about it, your opponents will help you sigh about your hard luck. Sympathy is all you get.

Many years ago, one of the Lords Yarborough of England would bet a thousand pounds to one before any deal that a particular player would not be dealt a hand with no ace, face card or ten-spot. That was the time to be alive! If you got one of those hands when Lord Yarborough was around, and if you had made the bet before the deal, you would collect a thousand pounds.

Actually, Lord Yarborough was not a philanthropist. The true odds against holding a hand with no card higher than a nine are 1827 to 1. If the noble lord made enough bets he probably collected a darned sight more than he paid out.

BRIDGE EXPERT MUST BE ROGUE

When people say bridge is a very scientific game I never raise my voice to protest. After all, that makes me some kind of scientist, and scientists rate pretty high these days.

My conscience keeps nagging me, however. Contract bridge is far from all science. Low cunning plays a very important part. There, I've said it. A bridge expert is not always a scientist; sometimes he's just a rogue.

If there is no larceny in your make-up you cannot rise to the heights of bridgedom. The true expert must be able to steal during the bidding and during the play, with the left hand as well as the right.

Cue Bidding

You can see this very clearly in cue bidding. Your opponent bids a spade, and his partner bids three spades. Now the opener bids four clubs, trying for a slam. He probably has the ace of clubs, perhaps other high clubs as well.

If the opening bidder is a painfully honest man you won't lead a club against him. You'll be looking for the weak spot, and you'll know that clubs is not the suit.

Isn't that helpful? Aren't you happy to have a reliable opponent?

Life is tougher when your opponent is the sort of hardened sinner who will sometimes make a cue bid in his weakest suit. When he bids four clubs he may have two small clubs instead of something like A-Q.

Mind you, life is still a bed of roses if your opponent is so crooked that you can rely on him to be up to no good. When that sort of opponent bids clubs, you lead clubs.

The real trouble comes when you have the kind of opponent who mixes 'em up. Sometimes he has the merchandise, and sometimes he doesn't.

Your struggle against this sort of player is not purely scientific; it's a battle of wits. You must try to work out not only what his bids mean but also whether or not he is telling the truth. A knowledge of people may be just as useful as knowledge of the game.

Deceptive Play

The same principle applies in the play of the cards. For example, declarer will usually make an early play in the suit that interests him most. The defenders can usually afford to leave this suit alone, concentrating their attack on the other suits.

Sound procedure against an "honest" declarer. But you must watch out for the rogue who makes a fake play in a suit he doesn't give a hoot about— and then waits for you to break the other suits for him.

You can't rely on mere science against opponents of this kind. You must fight fire with fire by becoming a scientific rascal.

HOW LONG TO THINK

Time is one of the big problems in world championship matches. How much time should a player be allowed for any single bridge hand?

Some years ago the late Ely Culbertson ordered a plate of spinach while he considered the play of a hand. He consumed the spinach, which presumably gave him the strength to think straight, and played the hand to a successful conclusion— after 45 minutes!

More recently, Bacherich and Ghestem, members of the French team, used long delays as a weapon against nervous opponents. In the 1954 world championship, at Monte Carlo, the Frenchmen took so long on

one hand that Billy Rosen, playing for America, fainted in his chair. Fortunately, smelling salts had been stocked by the tournament director, who was familiar with Ghestem's methods.

It Concerns You

You may wonder how this concerns you. After all, it may be years before you play in a world championship. With luck, you may escape it altogether.

Time is still a problem. Nobody takes 45 minutes to play a hand in a sociable game of bridge, but even 10 minutes may seem like an eternity. You can't always give a hand the consideration it really merits.

I remember the occasion when a friend of mine was declarer in a difficult hand at New York's famous Cavendish Club. He studied the dummy intently before calling for the first card, muttered "Excuse me —this will take another minute or two," and went on thinking.

The dummy went out to buy a newspaper, and one of the opponents stalked away to get a magazine. Ten minutes later, our hero played the first card. Dummy returned as the hand was over and asked how it had gone.

"It was a cold hand," declarer announced.

How many players could get away with that?

Not many; perhaps fortunately so. I like an unhurried pace, myself, but I like to see a card played every few minutes.

What Should You Do?

What should you do when you have a really difficult hand? Give it two or three minutes to see if inspiration comes. At the end of that time, stop stewing. Go ahead with one of the plans you have been considering. It may be as good as anything you could devise in the next hour.

Save your problem for a free hour—commuting, lunch or whatever. Maybe you'll discover the right way to handle all hands of that type.

If this doesn't help, dip into a bridge book. There are several very fine books, including a couple of my own, which will show you how to manage hands of many kinds. Invest a little time away from the table and you'll find that things go faster and better when you actually play.

HOW TO BE AN EXPERT

There's more to being a successful player than just knowing how to bid and play. All sorts of additional factors enter into the picture.

For example, one of the best-known stars of tournament bridge is a handsome man with distinguished-looking silver hair. Some of us, perhaps resentfully, think that half the women he plays against are happy to lose to such a handsome man; they give him bushels of tricks that even he never hoped to win.

I once suggested to my wife that I ought to go to a different barber to get some of this man's results. She gave me the look that every husband knows and told me it would be a waste of good money.

Belligerent Star

Another tournament star got good results for years by frightening timid opponents. He acted and looked very belligerent, and when he snarled a defiant notrump many an opponent would quail and lead a different suit. The unsoundness of his penalty doubles drove his partners to strong drink, but the amount of scorn he could pack into the word "Double" often produced a trick or two that were not in the cards.

We won't discuss the ladies who play in a mixed pair event dressed in some startling getup with a peekaboo blouse. Many's the hand I've had to play cross-eyed, but when I have to ask for blinkers to keep my mind on the game it will be time to retire from competition.

Time and Fatigue

Time and fatigue may, however, take your mind off the game. That's when an alert and crafty opponent will put his fast one over the plate.

I well remember the semifinals of the national team championship a few years ago when I played "black on black" against one of the keenest players in the game. The hour was late, the contest had begun several days before, and everybody was tired. The contract was four spades, and declarer led a trump as soon as he won a trick. I "followed suit" with a club, neither too quickly nor too slowly.

Declarer would have noticed a heart or a diamond, but the black on black play got past him. He miscounted the trumps, went after an extra trick, and found a way to go down.

Red on red will work equally well. If you cannot follow *suit*, it will often pay you to follow *color*. This is not always the best play in theory, but in practice against a weary opponent it may be devastating.

Speed of play is another important factor. If you can snap out your cards with hardly a pause for breath, you can often induce the opponents to match your speed. It's not your fault if you know just what you're doing and they don't. If you're not a good fast player, don't try this stunt and don't let an opponent rush you into a thoughtless play.

THE ANCESTRY OF CONTRACT BRIDGE

We usually think of whist as the earliest game of the family, but it was preceded by a whole series of games. The first was known as triumph, which in the course of time became corrupted to trump. Then followed games known as ruff and honors, whisk and swabbers, whisk and finally whist.

All of these games developed in England. Nobody knows exactly when triumph was first played, but it is mentioned in books of the early sixteenth century. By Shakespeare's time, games of this type were well known, and Shakespeare makes several references to them.

Whist was studied as a scientific game by a group of gentlemen who met at the Crown Coffee House, London, early in the eighteenth century. Edmond Hoyle adopted their findings and added some of his own in his famous "Short Treatise on the Game of Whist," published in 1742.

Hoyle First Expert

Hoyle was the first of the great experts of card games, and his name has survived as a synonym for correctness and skill. We say "according to Hoyle" in referring to poker and other games that didn't even exist in Hoyle's lifetime.

The basic idea of whist is easy for bridge players to understand. The dealer turned up the last card to determine the trump suit. The player to his left made the first lead, and all four players took part in the play. There was no exposed dummy and no bidding.

Whist reigned until the 1890's, when a game called bridge was introduced on both sides of the Atlantic. In the new game the dealer could name a trump suit or notrump, or he could permit his partner to make the choice. The opening lead was made by the player at dealer's left, and the hand of dealer's partner was then exposed as the dummy.

Auction Bridge

After a reign of only about ten years, bridge was supplanted by auction bridge. This allowed all four players to take part in the selection of the trump suit. The highest bid determined the choice, much as in present contract bridge. The chief difference was that it wasn't necessary to bid games or slams to get credit for them.

After about 20 years, players on both sides of the Atlantic began to experiment with forms of the game in which a player had to bid game to get credit for making it. A game known as plafond developed in France in 1922, but contract bridge as we know it began in 1925, when Harold S. Vanderbilt invented it during a cruise between Los Angeles and Havana.

Contract bridge was first played by "socialites" and serious devotees of auction bridge. The game received a tremendous impetus through publicity stunts engineered by Ely Culbertson, notably the matches against Sidney Lenz and Mr. and Mrs. P. Hal Sims.

After more than 30 years, contract bridge is more popular than ever. Originally an Anglo-Saxon game, it has spread to all parts of the Western world and to the Near and Far East. In the United States alone there are several thousand bridge clubs, supported by a few million "regular" players, and estimates of "occasional" players run as high as 40 million.

A KIBITZER'S PARADISE

A world championship is a kibitzer's paradise. Hundreds of spectators watch every hand of an important match, bid by bid and play by play.

All of the cards are shown on a special illuminated board, with "cards" that can be seen even from the back of a large auditorium. Every bid is announced, and then chalked up on a blackboard. After the opening lead, the lights are turned out behind the cards that have been played.

One of the advantages of watching a match from an auditorium seat is that you can comment on the bidding and play without affecting the players; they are in a distant room, and all of their bids and plays are telephoned to the officials in the auditorium.

Another advantage is that you can express an opinion without waiting years to become a senior kibitzer. Even a dorbitzer can speak up.

Privileges of Rank

We live in a democratic age, and the distinctions and privileges of rank are disappearing all over the world, but many bridge players will be sorry to see the end of the graded kibitzer. In a good bridge club, you couldn't become a kibitzer just by paying your dues and sitting behind a player. You had to earn your laurels.

Sometimes you would sit silently and watch a game for months before anybody took any notice of you. If you played a single hand in the meantime, you would lose all your seniority and would have to start over.

If you stuck to it long enough, you would become recognized as a kibitzer. And then you could advise the players, sneer at their bidding and play, eat at the table and smear ketchup over the cards, and even snatch a card out of a player's hand if he took too long to play.

In the Golden Age of Kibitzing, a ranking kibitzer was often flanked by two or three dorbitzers. They stood up, while the kibitzer always had a seat of honor. Dorbitzers could never, of course, speak directly to a player but they could confer with other dorbitzers or offer a suggestion to the kibitzer.

There was even a rank lower than the dorbitzers—the tsitsers. They stood even farther from the table than the dorbitzers and couldn't say a word. They could merely click their tongues —"Ts-ts-ts" whenever they disagreed with a bid or a play.

All of these distinctions have vanished today. The man in the next seat at a world championship may mutter "Lead a spade, you idiot," and for all you know he may be a mere dorbitzer. Or even a tsitser.

Kibitzer's Advantage

People sometimes wonder why a kibitzer is right more often than a player. This may be true even when the kibitzer watches only one hand and even when that one hand is bid and played by an expert.

The kibitzer's advantage is that he doesn't have to commit himself. He can just sit in his chair and say nothing until the end of a hand. Then, if all has gone well, he can comment "That's just the way I'd have done it." But if the player has gone wrong on a close decision, the kibitzer can (and usually does) point out that he would have done something different.

Some people think of bridge as a game of pure reasoning, but I assure you that those cats are not hep. Reasoning plays an important part in bridge, but so does human nature. If you don't know people you can't rise to the heights in bridge.

Let's take a simple and common example. Your trump suit consists of K-J-10-9 in your own hand and A-7-6-5 in the dummy. Naturally, you plan to finesse for the queen.

Which way do you finesse? Do you lead the jack and let it ride for a finesse? Or do you lead to dummy's ace and finesse back in the other direction?

To the uninitiated, this looks like a guess, pure and simple. You have to guess which opponent has the queen, and then you finesse through that opponent.

There is guesswork in it, but it isn't simple and it's far from pure. A beginner will guess right about 50 per cent of the time because he's just guessing. An expert will capture the queen at least 80 per cent of the time, because he has more than guesswork to guide him.

The expert knows people.

Weak Opponents

Let's suppose you're playing against your Aunt Tillie and one of her lady friends. They play bridge once a month, and think it's almost as refined a game as euchre. If you misguess a queen against these opponents

you'd better take up tiddly-winks.

The proper play is to lead the jack of trumps and wait for a reaction. If Aunt Tillie wavers and doesn't know quite what to do, she has the queen of trumps and is trying to remember whether the rule says "Cover an honor," or "Don't cover." By the time she has made up her mind, you know where the queen is and have no further problem.

The reverse is equally important. If your Aunt Tillie plays a low trump without the slightest sign of being flustered, she doesn't have the queen. Go up with dummy's ace and take your finesse in the other direction.

Good Opponents

If your opponents are very experienced you won't get your information quite so easily. You can still get it, but it comes in a different way and you have to know what to look for.

For example, there are the tricky players who hesitate for a tiny fraction of a second before playing a low trump on your jack of trumps. It's so close to imperceptible that you can't really tell that it happened, except that you are left with the impression that this opponent has the queen. Of course he doesn't. Don't complain that such a player is unethical; just learn to recognize his little tricks.

The best opponents of all give

you nothing to go by. They play practically each card with the same motion and the same lack of emphasis. Such players exist, but they're rare. Most opponents are just people and you can read them if you get to know people.

HOW TO WIN THE POST MORTEM

There comes a time in almost every bridge game when the hostess brings out the coffee and cake. That's when the post mortems fly thick and fast, when praise and reproach are dealt out.

How do you handle the post mortem? Has anybody given you advice on this vital part of the game? Most of the textbooks carry you through bidding and play, but they leave you to your own devices just when you are most in need of expert advice.

Be Friendly

Always begin the post mortem with a friendly word of praise for your partner. "You played well tonight," may seem an uninspired beginning, but it is still much favored by experts.

"I've never seen you play so well," is much better, of course, particularly if your partner has actually played like a catfish with the blind staggers. With this one sentence you soothe your partner and make it clear to the opponents that your evening has been one long struggle.

Accuracy Pays

No matter how skillful you are, your partner will sometimes get the first word in.

"Where on earth did you find that last bid?" she may ask.

Now you must move quickly. Your partner doesn't expect an answer to this type of question; in fact, she is just leading up to her opinion of that bid and perhaps a few others. Let her get well started, and the post mortem is lost.

Tell her just where you found the bid in question. Don't just say you found it in a book. Name the book and give a page number. Incidentally, stay away from round numbers. There may actually be something very important on page 200 of a book, but page 187 sounds more convincing. Accuracy of this kind is very important.

Staging a Diversion

If your partner happens to be your spouse, you may have trouble with this page 187 routine. It wears a bit thin after the tenth time you have used it.

Be ready to divert attention to the opponents. Congratulate one of them, for example, on using the same kind of bid very successfully earlier in the evening. Then praise his partner for sizing up the situation correctly and making the correct decision.

By this time both opponents will be on your side, and your partner will be glad to join in a discussion of how well they handled the situation.

Naturally, you mustn't let your spouse see this column. I've already hidden it from mine.

HOW MUCH TO TALK

How much table talk is allowable during a bridge game?

Before you answer the question in your own mind, remember that there are two kinds of table talk. The first kind, which has nothing to do with the game, concerns where Mrs. Whoozis sends her laundry or why there is reason to believe Mrs. Whatzis will be heading for the divorce courts if she doesn't watch out.

This type of conversation is completely up to the players. I won't pretend that as a male I'm above mere gossip. I'm bored by laundry and shopping, but I'm delighted to hear the dirt about Mrs. Whatzis and her gallivanting. Even in a tournament, which must run on a tight schedule, there's often time for a joke or a choice item of news.

The second kind of table talk, which relates to the game, should be permitted only between deals. While a hand is in progress, you should never say anything that has to do with bridge.

Mind you, there are exceptions to this rule—especially in a very casual game. If you put up a high card in third position and want to murmur "Not through the Iron Duke," you may be asked to say something new once in a while, but nobody will feel injured.

No Time for Lessons

The important thing to remember is that the middle of a bridge hand is no time to give your partner lessons. If you don't like his bidding or his play, wait until the end of a hand before you say a word. (And even then say nothing, if you want my advice.)

Let's consider conversational crimes to see why they're wrong. Suppose the dealer opens with a shutout bid of three hearts. The next two players pass, and it's up to you. You have a fairly good hand, good enough for a game if your partner has a few kings and queens. The danger is that he may have a very bad hand, and then you'll be slaughtered if you step in.

You have no problem if your partner can urge you on conversationally. For example, he may say "Faint heart never won fair lady," and you will know he wants you to bid. But if he sits quietly in his chair, you may reasonably deduce that he is too weak to offer any encouragement. Obviously this kind of conversational signal is unfair to the opponents.

The same kind of thing may happen in the play of the cards. You make an opening lead in good faith, and your partner scowls horribly and asks, "Whatsamatter, didncha hear my bid?" It's clear that he wants you to lead his suit the next time you have the chance. If he had said nothing, you might think of continuing your own suit.

Talk across the table in this fashion amounts to robbing the opponents. If you have to talk during a bridge hand, stick to gossip and say nothing about the game.

THREE LITTLE WORDS

There are hundreds of things to think about when you play bridge even if you manage to suppress the worries that bother most of us, such as "Is my partner annoyed because of the way I botched the last hand?" or "Can everybody see that I spilled ice cream on my lap at dinner?" Even if you manage to concentrate on the business at hand, you may still have too much to think about.

If you were a machine, you could cover everything on every hand; the wheels would go 'round, every possibility would be considered, and you would make a move once every two minutes or so. At that rate you would play a hand every half-hour, and you'd have time to oil the machinery when you were dummy.

Unfortunately, this pace might make the other players restless. "The chess club is on the other side of town," one of them would tell you; or somebody might ask you to blink now and then to make it clear you were still alive.

Must Compromise

Since nobody can possibly think of everything, we all have to compromise. We try to think of the most important things.

If you're declarer, the important thing is to make your contract. If you're a defender, the important thing is to defeat the contract. Everything else is secondary.

An experienced declarer studies the dummy when the opening lead has been made. He counts his tricks and looks for ways to get whatever additional tricks are required for the contract. Everybody expects declarer to plan his play in this fashion; in fact, he would be considered a shirker if he didn't.

Strangely enough, however, nobody expects a defender to do his share of the work. It's just as important, but only experts do it.

Mind you, there's nothing mysterious about good defense. You could average about a thousand points per session better than you do now if you always defended with these three words in mind: *Count your tricks.*

Let's take a simple example. You are defending against a contract of four spades. Your first thought should be: "We need four tricks to defeat this contract."

Your next step is to look in your hand to see how many of

[143]

these four tricks will come from your own hand. If you can see the four tricks in your own hand, make sure you get 'em. The world is full of players who fell asleep when the time came to take the setting trick.

If you cannot defeat the contract singlehanded, count the number of tricks you need from your partner. Then look for a way to get that number of tricks.

Aimless defense will get you nowhere. Aim for a definite number of tricks and always keep that number in mind as you plan your play.

This is simpler and faster than getting a machine to play the hand for you—and very nearly as effective.

BRIDGE PLAYER HAS LIMITED VOCABULARY

What should you say during a bridge game?

It depends on you, the other players, and the nature of the game. Some games are decorous, others are ribald; the conversation may be polite or rude; and what you can say may depend partly on how big the other fellow is.

Still, there is a right and a wrong time to talk. From the time you pick up your cards until the play of the last trick you should limit all the talk to a vocabulary of exactly 15 words:

Pass, double, redouble.

One, two, three, four, five, six, seven.

Notrump, spades, hearts, diamonds, clubs.

End of vocabulary. Nothing more.

Forbidden Words

Do not say "Bye" or "Bye me" when you mean "pass." Don't say "I'll pass." Don't say "Content," when an opponent doubles. The single word "Pass" is enough for *all* these situations.

There may be one exception to this rule. An Englishman's "Pahss" rounds like "Hearts," and for this reason the English say "No bid." If you have an English or Bostonian accent, it's quite all right to say "No bid" whenever you pass. It would be wrong to say "No bid" some of the time and "Pass" at other times.

The same principle holds for the other bids. "One club" is correct. "I'll bid a club" is improper. "Three spades" is correct. "The third spade" is improper.

The trouble with the forbidden words and phrases is that most of us are creatures of habit. When a player bids "The third spade" he always has a poor hand; he never wants his partner to go on to four spades. But when he bids "three spades" he has sound values and is hopeful of hearing more from his partner.

This sort of bidding distinction is foreign to the spirit of the game. All bids of three spades should sound alike.

These rules are broken in millions of home games throughout the continent. It doesn't matter much because all the offenders are completely unaware of wrongdoing, and their opponents all do the same thing. In a serious game with experienced players, however, a player who uses the wrong phrases encounters the raised eyebrow and the curled lip.

Think nothing of it if your regular game is highly sociable and not very serious. But stick to the approved 15 words if you play with a new group or with experienced players.

THE UNLUCKY EXPERT

How well do you know the Unlucky Expert? He's a member of every bridge club, perhaps of even smaller groups. Don't look now, but you're standing close to a mirror . . .

The Unlucky Expert was first isolated for science by S. J. Simon in 1945, in his classic book *Why You Lose at Bridge.* "His bidding is perfect," Simon commented, "his play flawless. But he never wins. All his partners let him down."

Simon showed the Unlucky Expert in action. His partner opened with one spade, and our hero had a very good hand—five good spades, five strong hearts, and A-K-x of diamonds. Unfortunately, he had no clubs at all.

Why this should be unfortunate may not be clear unless you know how often accidents happen to the Unlucky Expert. He bid his hand very scientifically in his attempt to get to seven spades. But somehow or other he got dropped in a contract of six clubs.

As so often happens, our hero's partner was not a scientist. He didn't understand what was going on, so he passed the first bid that seemed comfortable. Down seven at six clubs, with seven spades absolutely laydown!

Still With Us

We don't have to go back 18 years or read books to find the Unlucky Expert. He is still with us. In fact, with all the new bidding gadgets that have come along in the last few years, his tribe has increased more than ever.

Just the other night, I saw the Unlucky Expert get to a contract of five spades that most of us would miss. It was a long, muddled auction, with a Blackwood bid of four notrump at one stage. Our hero's partner, an earnest young lady who had been playing for almost six months, made the correct response of five hearts to show two aces. Then the Unlucky Expert bid five spades, and everybody passed. It was the first time spades had been bid.

Of course you know what the Unlucky Expert meant. He wanted his partner to bid five notrump, which he would pass. But then, you're not an earnest young lady. Or perhaps you've been playing bridge for more than six months.

The Unlucky Expert is usually allowed to play his ad-

[145]

venturous contracts undoubled. That's because his opponents can't believe how unlucky the poor fellow is. If they doubled him, he might redouble! The redouble asks for a takeout, of course. But you know how accidents happen.

While we're on the subject, how's your own luck these days? Are your partners letting you down?

THE SURE-THING BET

"Is it proper to bet on a sure thing?" asks a reader.

Why, the very idea! It's considered unsporting to bet on a sure thing, especially if the amount of the bet is small. Big bets are another thing, as we'll soon see.

"One of the men at the bridge club offered to bet me on a bridge hand," my correspondent continues. "He's willing to bet quite a lot, and he's sure to lose. Still, he's nobody's fool. Here's the hand:

♠ 5 4 3 2   ♡ 4 3 2
♢ 4 3 2   ♣ 4 3 2

"You're on lead against seven notrump, this bird says, and you lead fourth-best from your longest and strongest—the deuce of spades. Later, you win a trick with the five of spades. He says there is no revoke, no lead out of turn, no trick taken in error—that the five of spades wins a trick perfectly properly and legally.

"He wants to bet that this is possible, and I'm quite sure he's out of his mind. Should I take his bet?"

Betting Is Wrong

I cannot conscientiously advise a reader to bet. Many of my readers have strong moral objections to betting, and I wouldn't dream of offending them. Besides, in this case, my reader is not on the right end of a sure-thing bet; he's on the *wrong* end!

It's a strange hand. How can you possibly win a trick with that five of spades? It cannot be a trick that somebody else leads to, for nobody can lead a spade lower than the five. It cannot be a trick that you lead to, since you cannot gain the lead.

Suppose each of the other players has three spades. Declarer has all the aces, kings and queens, with one jack. He wins the first spade, leads out the ace of hearts and accidentally plays a second heart on this trick. Nobody notices this little accident for a trick or two, until suddenly declarer notices that he has one card less than anybody else.

It is now too late to correct the situation; he must play on with his deficient hand. Eventually, he wins the twelfth trick with his last card and everybody else has one card. The lead now passes to his left.

And this is where the five of spades wins a trick!

There's a moral to this little tale. Don't make a big bet on a sure thing. The chances are your opponent knows some little gimmick that you haven't thought of. You'll lose your bet, and you'll look foolish in the bargain.

If somebody offered to bet me that he could make the king of hearts jump out of the deck and squirt ketchup over my face, I might make a small bet on the proposition—but only because I have a lively curiosity and happen to like the taste of ketchup.

THE UNLUCKIEST HAND

You probably wouldn't consider it a misfortune to pick up 13 spades, but I know several people who remember it with regret.

No, this isn't the story of bidding seven spades only to have the player at your left bid seven notrump. That was 13 hearts, and everybody knows that hearts and spades are not the same thing.

You want to know about the 13 hearts also? It was presented as a problem in the World Bridge Olympics almost 30 years ago. If you bid seven hearts all at once and redoubled furiously, you made it obvious that you had all 13 hearts. So then your left-hand opponent bid seven notrump and made it.

If you were cagy, you bid only two hearts to start with. Some experts passed. Some started with one diamond! Eventually you got to seven hearts, doubled—but not redoubled. Think of the fun of bidding up to the slam gradually, allowing the opponents to push you to seven!

Spades Were Tougher

The perfect spade hand was unluckier. It was dealt out in a duplicate game at the Mildred Lovejoy Studio a year or two after the perfect heart hand had appeared in the Olympics. (Actually, it was prepared in advance; nobody could have dealt this hand out.)

The dealer had 13 spades. By a curious coincidence *so did everybody else at the table!* Just think of how all the experts tried to bid cagily, allowing themselves to get pushed to seven spades.

Eventually, somebody got to seven spades doubled. And then Miss Lovejoy would appear on the scene as soon as the opening lead and the sight of the dummy made it clear that the deck consisted of 52 spades. "Play it out," she would say. "Spades are trumps. If two of you play the same card on a trick, the earlier one wins."

In the course of the evening more than 50 people held 13 spades and could take only six or seven tricks at a spade contract! That was a very unlucky hand.

There were other strange hands in that duplicate game. One of them had no aces, but four extra deuces scattered around so that nobody could tell during the bidding that the deck had been tampered with. I remember that Sonny Moyse, editor of The Bridge World, and his partner, Mitch Barnes, also a famous expert, managed to bid up to six notrump. Sonny did seem a bit disappointed when he saw the dummy.

It's pleasant to poke the fire after a hearty Christmas dinner and think back to the days when men were men and didn't bid like pantywaists!

MAN OR MOUSE?

There comes a time in every bridge player's life when he must decide whether he is a man or a mouse. I am here to squeak that you'll live longer as a mouse. Happier, too.

Just a few weeks ago, a friend of mine passed his partner at three clubs redoubled. It could happen only to a brave man, not to a mouse.

The auction was confused, beginning with one club—bid by an opponent. When my friend's partner eventually bid three clubs it was hard to tell whether he really had clubs or wanted to be taken out.

When the smoke had cleared —2,600 points worth of smoke —it turned out that the partner had wanted to be taken out.

Rules for Mice

This could never happen if two of the players at the table followed my Rules for Mice:

1. Don't redouble unless your partner is sure to know exactly what you mean.

2. Don't pass a redouble unless you know exactly what your partner means.

3. When in doubt, take a profit.

Take Your Profit

In many competive bidding situations you must choose between bidding on and doubling the opponents. If you can't be sure of the right course, do whatever is most likely to give you a plus score of some kind.

The theory is very simple: If you get a plus score on every hand, at the end of the evening you won't be a loser. Ask any mathematician, or try it for yourself on one of those giant computing machines.

If the double looks very safe, sit back and collect. If the double looks very doubtful, settle for a modest contract of your own. It's neither necessary nor wise to aim for the maximum score on every single hand.

OPENING LEADS VARY WITH AGE

Which card should you lead when you hold three small cards of your partner's suit? Should you lead the highest or the lowest of the three cards?

The answer depends, in part, on the date of your birth, your latitude and longitude, and on how seriously you play bridge. If that's not enough, add your partner's age and what everybody has had for dinner.

If I were kidding, this wouldn't be a very good joke. This is actually a serious discussion of how you pick the "right" lead.

Twenty or thirty years ago, all of the experts agreed on this point. If you held 8-7-4 of your partner's suit you led the eight. That was that, and no arguments.

The disagreement began to appear in the last ten or fifteen years. The younger experts in the United States and Canada began to favor the opening lead of the *lowest* card rather than the highest.

If you don't take bridge very seriously, this may sound like an argument between Tweedledum and Tweedledee. You can go right on leading the highest card of partner's bid suit just as you have done in the past. As long as you're consistent about it, you'll continue to get good results.

Advantages of Change

If you do take bridge seriously, you'll wonder why the younger experts favor a change. They lead the top card of partner's suit when they have only two such cards (or perhaps only one). When they lead low, they show three or more cards of partner's suit.

The younger experts say that it's important for your partner to know when you have a doubleton.

Let's suppose you lead the eight of his suit. If you're playing the old-fashioned way, partner knows that you may have a doubleton or three cards of his suit. (We'll disregard singletons for the moment.) Your partner may have a hard time deciding which it is, especially if declarer is a shrewd false-carder.

If you're playing the Modern Scientific style, the lead of the eight tells partner that you have only two cards of his suit. If you had three or more, you would lead low. The certainty that you have a short holding in his suit may be all-important.

Against this we have to balance a disadvantage. When an old-fashioned player leads the lowest card of his partner's suit, he promises four small cards or perhaps three to an honor. When the New Scientist leads the lowest card of his partner's suit, he may have three very small cards. The partner cannot tell whether it is three or four.

Now, what was all this nonsense about latitude and longitude and your partner's age?

The important thing is to lead in such a way that your partner knows what you are doing. Even if you are young enough to be a New Scientist, it will pay to defer to your partner if he prefers the old-fashioned leads. Your own age and your partner's age will probably be an important factor in which way you decide to lead.

The new leads are well established in expert circles in the United States and Canada but not elsewhere. That's why geography would have something to do with your leads.

WHATEVER YOUR INTEREST, or perhaps your hobby, look over this list of many wonderful and interesting **REFERENCE BOOKS**

We're sure you will find a number that will be of interest and will help you.

☐ **NR 2** **ALL NEW FANNIE FARMER BOSTON COOKING SCHOOL COOK**
(95¢) **BOOK, Wilma Lord Perkins.** More than 3,000 mouth-watering recipes, old favorites as well as new. Step-by-step directions including sections on packaged and frozen foods, and mixes. Every recipe tested so that no matter what equipment is used, it will be perfect. Included are charts, tables, menus and attractive illustrations.

☐ **SR 3** **TRAVEL GUIDE TO EUROPE: BRITISH ISLES AND WESTERN**
(75¢) **EUROPE, Myra Waldo.** When the destination is Austria, Switzerland or any other Western country, here is the book for travelers. Information on when to go, how to go, hotels, restaurants, foreign phrases, costs, etc. are included. Also currency charts, tipping guides, sample itineraries and points of interest. A "must" for any traveler.

☐ **SR 4** **TRAVEL GUIDE TO EUROPE: THE MEDITERRANEAN AND**
(75¢) **NORTHERN EUROPE, Myra Waldo.** This book gives travelers all the necessary information on journeying to Portugal, Spain, Italy, Yugoslavia, Greece, Russia, Finland, Sweden and Norway. Information on when to go, how to go, hotels, restaurants, foreign phrases, costs, etc., are included. Also currency charts, tipping guides, sample itineraries and points of interest.

☐ **SR 6** **FIELD GUIDE TO EARLY AMERICAN FURNITURE, Thomas H.**
(75¢) **Ormsbee.** The basic book for antique buyers, describing how to identify every period, when and where the furniture was made, and how much to pay. Over 350 illustrations are included in this indispensable guide.

☐ **NR 7** **FUCILLA SPANISH DICTIONARY, Joseph G. Fucilla.** The most
(95¢) complete English to Spanish, Spanish to English dictionary in paperback. Over 60,000 entries, including the latest terms, all in a modern, easy-to-use format. It also contains keys to pronunciation, and a huge selection of idioms, phrases and expressions.

☐ **NR 9** **SOULE'S DICTIONARY OF ENGLISH SYNONYMS, Richard Soule.**
(95¢) The standard work for finding the proper word—unsurpassed in completeness, simplicity and handiness. It is arranged in dictionary style and contains over 20,000 word entries. The biggest paperback word-finder in existence.

☐ **FR 10** **MYTHS AND LEGENDS OF ALL NATIONS, Herbert S. Robinson &**
(50¢) **Knox Wilson.** A practical guide to the mythologies, religions and philosophies of the world. The exciting stories of over 2,000 mythological figures from the ancient worlds of Egypt and Greece to contemporary America. Wonderful tales of love, adventure and folklore.

☐ **HR 11** **A NEW TREASURY OF FOLK SONGS, Tom Glazer.** The best of the
(60¢) world's great folk songs, from ballads and spirituals to sea chanties,
etc. Here are the most authentic versions complete with words and
music. All the old favorites are found in the up-to-date edition.
An extra dividend is the inclusion of Mr. Glazer's easy beginner
lessons on playing the guitar.

☐ **HR 12** **GETTING ALONG IN SPANISH, Mario Pei and Eloy Vaquero.** Con-
(60¢) venient language guides for the traveler or student. More than
1100 ready-to-use everyday phrases, plus a basic vocabulary which
will enable the beginner to cope with any foreign language problem.

☐ **HR 13** **GETTING ALONG IN FRENCH, Mario Pei and John Fisher.** Con-
(60¢) venient language guides for the traveler or student. More than
1100 ready-to-use everyday phrases, plus a basic vocabulary which
will enable the beginner to cope with any foreign language problem.

☐ **HR 14** **GETTING ALONG IN ITALIAN, Mario Pei.** Convenient language
(60¢) guides for the traveler or student. More than 1100 ready-to-use
everyday phrases, plus a basic vocabulary which will enable the
beginner to cope with any foreign language problem.

☐ **HR 15** **GETTING ALONG IN GERMAN, Mario Pei and Robert Politzer.**
(60¢) Convenient language guides for the traveler or student. More than
1100 ready-to-use everyday phrases, plus a basic vocabulary which
will enable the beginner to cope with any foreign language problem.

☐ **NR 16** **AKHMANOVA RUSSIAN DICTIONARY, O. S. Akhmanova.** The
(95¢) finest Russian-English English-Russian dictionary in any low-priced
edition. Contains a comprehensive and up-to-date listing of 60,000
entries; a simplified Russian pronunciation key; and a wide selection of idioms, phrases and expressions.

☐ **HR 17** **COLLECTORS' GUIDE TO STANDARD U. S. COINS, Herbert P.
(60¢) Ferguson.** A collector's guide to standard U. S. coins which coin
collectors will recognize as an indispensable addition to their
libraries. Complete with pictures, dates, and latest values of thousands of coins.

☐ **HR 18** **NEW WAYS IN SEX EDUCATION, Dr. Dorothy Walter Baruch.**
(60¢) This book contains all that a parent or teacher needs to know to
assist children to a normal sexual development. Dr. Baruch is a
nationally known psychologist and the author of over twenty books
in the field of adult and child psychology.

☐ **HR 20** **GETTING ALONG IN RUSSIAN, Mario Pei and Fedor I. Nikanov.**
(60¢) Convenient language guides for the traveler or student. More than
1100 ready-to-use everyday phrases, plus a basic vocabulary which
will enable the beginner to cope with any foreign language problem.

☐ **HR 26** **THE ART OF FRENCH COOKING, Fernande Garvin.** More than 200
(60¢) recipes from the world famous cuisine of France are included in
this mouth-watering book. The names are a roll call of succulence
—boeuf bourguignon, quiche Lorraine, garbure, piperade, tour-
nedos morateur, and many, many more.

☐ **HR 27** **THE ART OF ITALIAN COOKING, Maria LoPinto.** Here is the
(60¢) world's finest collection of the best recipes of the rich zestful
traditional foods of Italy—antipasto to zabaglione. More than 200
delicious, easily prepared dishes of authentic Italian cookery, complete with a handy glossary of terms.